DINNER
like a BOSS

DINNER
like a
BOSS

KATY HOLDER

hardie grant books

CONTENTS

LEGEND

- 🐟 Fish & seafood
- 🥕 Vegetarian or vegetarian option

INTRODUCTION

To my bonkers boys Max and Jack –
my very own ratbags. You keep me
young, yet turn my hair grey! Hand in
hand with your gorgeous dad, Alex,
you are truly the lights of my life.

I'm a busy working mum of two boys aged 11 and 13, and the recipes in this book are a collection of our family's favourites – along with lots of ideas that my boys and their friends thought should be in the book, all tested on my family and the local kids and families in our neighbourhood. All recipes are broken up into easy-to-follow steps and include quick-reference preparation and cooking times:

Serves/makes   Preparation time   Cooking time

I may not be the toughest of mums when it comes to making my kids eat, but I'm certainly no push-over. I have consistently encouraged them to try new foods and flavours. More importantly, I never give them an option for their dinner or cook more than one meal. Dinner is the same for all members of the family, but with tweaks here and there – I love to mix things up and try new additions to old favourites. And this is what I hope to give you with this book: inspiration for dishes that will allow you to get your family to sit down for dinner and enjoy (almost) the same meal together – with plenty of room for variation and optional extras to suit everybody's tastes and preferences. I hope you find lots of meals for your family and, over time, introduce your kids to a variety of dishes and flavours.

Here's to happy meal times!

Katy

Eat as a family

We all lead pretty busy lives and sometimes it can be hard to sit down as a family; and maybe after a long day it is the last thing you want to do. However, I try to eat dinner with my kids most nights. Not only is this a great time to find out what they did at school that day, but also I can see exactly what they are eating and – equally importantly – they get to see me eating and enjoying a wide range of foods. They also learn good table manners, and if Dad or other adults are eating with us they learn the art of respectful table conversation. Now that they are a bit older, they are definitely less fussy and are very aware of what a good balanced diet is, so the dinnertime battle is certainly less intense than it used to be. If you're still in the middle of it, hang on in there – for the majority it gets better.

Complete meals

What makes this book a little different is that I've tried to make every recipe, with the exception of the light meals, a complete meal: each dish contains protein, carbohydrates and plenty of vegetables, so you don't have to think about the accompaniments – everything you need for the meal i in the one recipe.

Options, options, options!

In any family, it's unlikely that every family member is going to like the same things at the same time. Some flavours can take a bit of time to get used to. My recipes are written as complete meals, but I've included lots of options for those with more adventurous tastes, and I'm talking about both kids and adults! Some flavourings like chilli, herbs, citrus and garlic may take time to be liked, but this doesn't mean that the rest of the family should miss out or, more importantly, that you should stop offering them to your kids. Equally, you don't want to waste a plate of food if your child really doesn't want to eat chilli, so instead of including it in the finished dish, put the suggested options in small bowls on the table and repeatedly encourage your kids to try them. With herbs, I encourage my kids to smell big bunches while I'm preparing them to teach them what they look, taste and smell like (we also grow herbs in the garden, so they can pick a leaf or three whenever they want). I also don't use herbs just as a garnish; they are usually an integral part of the dish.

Variations

Many of my recipes give variations to suit your family. I've included meat additions to vegetarian recipes, and also suggested how to make many of the meat recipes vegetarian or vegan.

Cooking yummy pizza with a little friend.

Kids and vegetables

I'm not sure why so many kids have a thing about vegetables when they never have an issue with ice cream and chocolate! How can a whole category of food be so vehemently rejected? For my family, not eating vegetables has never been an option – I really believe that you just have to keep on encouraging your kids to try them. So yes, I hide vegetables! There are several reasons for this. When my kids were younger, they were absolutely adamant that they wouldn't eat, for example, zucchini (courgette) or mushrooms. So the easiest way to get them to eat the veg anyway was to hide finely grated or finely chopped vegetables in meatballs, dumplings, burgers and kofta. After a while, when I knew they loved the food, I would tell them they had been happily eating the vegetables for months without knowing, and even once they knew it never stopped them wanting those dishes again. In the case of zucchini (courgette) and mushrooms, my kids still find it hard to eat them as an individual ingredient, but will very happily eat them if they are 'hidden' – even when they know they are hidden. I agree that you shouldn't continually hide vegetables and not tell the kids (because how will they ever get to like vegetables this way?), but I think it's OK to do it every now and then.

Unusual ingredients

It can be hard to think up new ideas for dinner every night. I have tried to suggest some more unusual recipes and have included some more unusual ingredients, where to get them and how to use them in various dishes, so they don't end up languishing in the refrigerator or cupboard.

For many years, my older son, Max, thought that carrots were 'orange fries'. It was only when we were living overseas for a while and we had some friends come to stay that their son, who was Max's age (about four), got very confused and whispered rather too loudly, 'Mum, Max calls them orange fries, but they are carrots ...' And the cat (or rather the carrot) was out of the bag. But we never looked back and he continues to love carrots to this day.

Another reason I hid food was to avoid food wastage – there would be no food left on plates when the vegetables were hidden inside popular dishes, and hence no food had to be thrown out.

Raw vegetables

With the guidelines on fruit and vegetable consumption now sitting at five to nine portions daily, it can be tricky to get that much fruit and vegetables into your family, especially as it should really only be two fruits. One strategy I use is to hand out a bowl of raw vegetables, such as carrots, snow peas (mangetout) and sugar snap peas, before dinner. That way, a good portion of the meal can be eaten before you all sit down and it gets your kids into the habit of snacking on raw vegetables at other times of the day.

Separatist kids

'What is a separatist?' I hear you cry. Well, this is the term we chose for our oldest son, who couldn't bear different foods on his plate to touch. This even stretched to dishes were food is all combined, like fried rice and bolognaise. He would more than happily eat all the different components individually but he just couldn't eat them all mixed up. It was more like a slight phobia than him just being fussy. To get around it and not have to cook different meals for him – which is something I have never done – I would cook the different ingredients individually and then serve his up separately on a plate and combine ours. I rarely pander to my kids' fussy food requirements, but this one I felt was a genuine issue for him, and as long as he was eating the ingredients in one form or another I was happy – and so was he. Gradually, I started combining the food or making it touch on his plate and slowly, slowly he ate the same as us and now he has totally grown out of it and eats pretty much everything (except mushrooms, at least knowingly ...). Encouraging kids to eat salads (especially substantial ones like pasta and rice salads) and mixed up food from a young age is a good way to introduce them to a combination of different flavours and textures. However, if you have a 'separatist' kid, the good thing about most salads is that they can also be served as individual components for those who want it and then all tossed together for everyone else. This way, you don't have to cook separate meals and can keep everyone happy, plus seeing the rest of the family eating their food combined might get the separatists to try it too, one day (generally most come round eventually).

Getting kids to eat fish

Getting kids to eat seafood can be tricky. Many kids really don't like the smell of fish, and a visit to the fishmongers can be quite overwhelming. I started my kids on white fish poached in milk, which, fortunately, they loved. I then gradually moved on to salmon and prawns. Initially, I also regularly served fish and prawns crumbed – it's rare that a kid refuses something that is crumbed!

Food textures

If your kids are struggling with the textures of some food, especially fish, try crumbing it. Once they are enjoying the fish, reduce the amount of crumb until they are happy just to eat the fish.

Everyone around the table: dinner with Alex, Jack and Max.

Portion sizes

When you look at your dinner plate it should look roughly like this: one half vegetables, one quarter protein and one quarter carbs. It's really important to ensure half the plate is vegetables.

Your portion sizes will depend on the size of your family and the age of your kids, but for pasta I tend to do 75 g (2¾ oz) per person, which is quite a bit less than the 100 g (3½ oz) suggested in many recipes. I make between 600 g–1 kg (1 lb 5 oz–2 lb 3 oz) of potatoes for the family (depending on how it's to be cooked – mash usually needs more), and I usually cook about 200 g (7 oz/1 cup) of rice. However, if you have hungry members of the family you may need to cook extra.

For meat and fish I serve around 150 g (5½ oz) per person. I think I am on the small side for meat and fish portions, because I prefer to fill up on vegetables – most of us really don't need that much meat in our lives (with the exception of growing teenage girls and boys).

I ensure we always have at least three different vegetables at dinner and quite often it is four. I accept that we may not achieve the suggested number of servings of vegetables every day, so instead of losing heart and feeling like we'll never achieve it, I try to stick rigidly to my own family's more achievable goal, adding extra whenever I can. This way I feel that we are well on the way to meeting the goals.

A few pantry staples

This is the selection of pantry staples that I like to have on hand:

Fish sauce
Soy sauce
Kecap manis (thick, sweetened soy sauce)
Honey
Balsamic vinegar
Red- and white-wine vinegars
Olive oil (for cooking)
Extra-virgin olive oil (for salads)
Vegetable oil (for cooking)
Sesame oil (for Asian food)
Ground cumin
Ground coriander
Dried oregano
Smoked paprika

Salt & pepper

Whenever I say to season to taste, I suggest you use sea salt flakes and freshly ground black pepper. For younger kids, you may choose not to add salt while cooking and instead have some on the table for the adults to add, if liked.

Personally, I don't like spray oils because they contain chemical propellants – have you ever wondered what that awful white stuff is that comes out when you spray?

Another great thing to have on hand in the fridge is chipotle chillies in adobo sauce – it is one of my favourites to add to soups, stews, pulled pork and chicken and marinades for fajitas and burritos. Chipotle chillies in adobo sauce aren't as spicy as many chillies. I like to use them for their smoky flavour rather than their heat, but having said that, if you add too many you will definitely feel the heat! Start with half a chilli and some of the sauce and then increase as your family gets used to them.

Vegan & vegetarian kids

If you have vegan kids coming to visit, any of the tofu recipes, including the Gado gado salad on page 34 (leave out the eggs) and the Zoodle recipe on page 63 with the Dairy-free pesto (page 64) should be winners. For vegetarians, keep a few vegetarian options (such as the Chickpea burgers on page 116) in the freezer to take the stress out of deciding what to cook for them.

Some notes on measurements

This book uses 20 ml (¾ fl oz) tablespoons and metric cup measurements: 1 cup = 250 g (9 oz).

LIGHT DISHES, SALADS, WRAPS & FLAT THINGS

If you're looking for a lighter meal or an appetiser or snack, or you are after food that doesn't need cutlery – think rice paper rolls or pizza ('flat things') – then check out the dishes in this chapter. I have also included several substantial salads, suitable for lunch or dinner.

10 rolls   30 minutes (or less if everyone makes their own)   5 minutes

Chicken and noodle rice paper rolls with hoisin-peanut sauce

These rolls will take about 30 minutes to make. However, if you get the family involved it will be quicker. Arrange the filling ingredients on a plate, then get the kids to assemble their own rolls. I doubt they will be perfectly rolled, but it really doesn't matter. One word of advice: don't put too much filling in each wrapper or you will have trouble rolling them. You may need to do the softening of the wrappers yourself – they can tear easily.

1 boneless, skinless chicken breast (about 250 g/9 oz), preferably free-range
50 g (1¾ oz) vermicelli noodles
1 Lebanese (short) cucumber
10 rice paper wrappers
10 small baby cos (romaine) lettuce leaves
1 medium carrot, peeled and cut into long thin matchsticks (about 5–6 cm/2–2½ in long)
handful of coriander (cilantro) leaves (optional)
1 tablespoon crushed peanuts, to serve

Hoisin-peanut sauce

70 g (2½ oz) crunchy peanut butter
3 tablespoons hoisin sauce
2 teaspoons soy sauce
1 teaspoon sugar
80 ml (2½ fl oz/⅓ cup) hot water

1 Cut the chicken breast in half horizontally to make two thinner steaks. To do this, place your hand flat on top of the chicken and use a sharp knife to slice through, horizontally. Put the chicken in a medium saucepan and add water to just cover. Place the lid on the pan and bring to a simmer. Simmer for 2 minutes, then remove the pan from the heat and leave the chicken to finish poaching in the water for 15 minutes. Drain the chicken, then shred it using two forks.

2 Meanwhile, put the noodles in a heatproof bowl, cover with boiling water and leave to soften for 6–8 minutes, then drain, or cook them according to the packet instructions. Rinse the noodles under cold running water to prevent them sticking together. Drain well, then, using scissors, cut the noodles into shorter lengths and put them in a bowl.

3 While the chicken is poaching, cut the cucumber in half lengthways and scoop out the seeds using a teaspoon. Cut the cucumber into thin batons about the same length as the carrot matchsticks.

4 One at a time, dip the rice paper wrappers briefly (for 10–20 seconds) in a large shallow bowl of warm water. Do not leave them in for too long or they may tear.

5 Place a wrapper on a board and place a lettuce leaf across the middle, one-third up from the bottom closest to you. Top with some noodles, carrot, cucumber and a few pieces of chicken. Top with several coriander leaves (if using). Fold the bottom of the wrapper over the filling, fold in the sides, then roll the parcel up quite tightly. Repeat with the remaining wrappers, keeping the prepared ones under some damp paper towel to prevent them drying out.

6 For the hoisin-peanut sauce, combine all the ingredients in a medium bowl. Divide the sauce between one or two smaller serving dishes. Sprinkle the peanuts over the sauce and serve the rice paper rolls with the sauce for dipping.

Variations

There are a number of different filling options to choose from. You can replace the chicken with cooked, peeled prawns (shrimp), halved lengthways, or strips of firm tofu or barbecued duck. You could also use leftover roast chicken, beef or pork (you'll need about 140 g/5 oz), strips of capsicum (bell pepper) or chunks of avocado. Large fresh mint leaves add a delicious flavour too, if liked.

12 fritters · 15 minutes · 30 minutes

Colourful vegetable and haloumi fritters with lemon and garlic mayonnaise

Fritters (savoury pancakes) are generally loved by all kids because they can pick them up with their hands. For a lighter meal, serve just the fritters with mayonnaise. For something more substantial, add some chunky home-made chips (fries) or wedges, and a salad or some cherry tomatoes and cucumber batons. If you don't want to serve the lemon and garlic mayonnaise, you can substitute it with plain good-quality whole egg mayonnaise.

2 zucchini (courgettes), about 350 g (12½ oz) in total, coarsely grated

2 carrots, about 250–300 g (9–10½ oz) in total, peeled and coarsely grated

250 g (9 oz) haloumi

2 eggs, lightly beaten

30 g (1 oz/½ cup) panko breadcrumbs

75 g (2¾ oz/½ cup) plain (all-purpose) flour

2 tablespoons finely chopped flat-leaf (Italian) parsley (optional)

2–3 tablespoons olive oil

Lemon and garlic mayonnaise

1 lemon

125 g (4½ oz/½ cup) good-quality whole egg mayonnaise

½ small garlic clove, crushed (optional)

pinch of sea salt

1 Preheat the oven to 180°C (350°F)/160°C (320°F) fan-forced and line a baking tray with baking paper. Put the grated zucchini and carrots in a clean tea towel (dish towel) and squeeze out as much liquid as possible. Alternatively, use clean hands to squeeze out the liquid. Put the grated vegetables in a large bowl.

2 Coarsely grate the haloumi and add it to the bowl, along with the egg. Beat the mixture with a spatula until well combined. Add the panko breadcrumbs, flour and parsley (if using) and season with salt and pepper to taste. Mix to combine.

3 Heat 2 tablespoons of the olive oil in a large frying pan over a medium heat. Take heaped tablespoonfuls of the mixture, place them in the pan and flatten slightly. Fry in batches for 3–4 minutes on each side, or until golden and almost cooked through. If the fritters are browning too quickly, reduce the heat. Transfer the fritters to the prepared tray and bake in the oven for a further 5–10 minutes, or until cooked through.

4 While the fritters are in the oven, make the lemon and garlic mayonnaise. Squeeze the juice from half the lemon and cut the remaining half into wedges. Combine the mayonnaise with 3–4 teaspoons of lemon juice (to taste), the garlic (if using) and sea salt.

5 Serve the fritters with the lemon and garlic mayonnaise, and any other accompaniments you like, with the lemon wedges for squeezing over.

Recipe image on page 22

Ricotta and pumpkin fritters

If you are keen to add some superfoods to your family's diet, incorporating quinoa flakes into these puffy fritters (savoury pancakes) is a great way to start. Alternatively, panko breadcrumbs, or even fresh breadcrumbs from day-old bread, work well too. This recipe is also a great way to use up leftover cooked pumpkin.

2–3 tablespoons olive oil
400 g (14 oz) butternut pumpkin (squash) or any other kind of pumpkin
2 teaspoons picked thyme leaves (optional)
350 g (12½ oz) firm ricotta
1 egg, lightly beaten
60 g (2 oz) quinoa flakes or panko breadcrumbs
200 g (7 oz/1⅓ cups) frozen peas, defrosted
1 long red chilli, seeded and finely chopped (optional)
sweet chilli sauce to serve (optional)

1. Preheat the oven to 220°C (430°F)/200°C (400°F) fan-forced. Put 1 tablespoon of the oil in a baking dish and put the dish in the oven to heat up. Peel and seed the pumpkin, cut it into 1–2 cm (½–¾ in) pieces, then put it in the baking dish. Season with salt and pepper and scatter over the thyme (if using). Toss to combine, then roast for 20–25 minutes, or until soft. Reduce the oven temperature to 170°C (340°F)/150°C (300°F) fan-forced.

2. Put the pumpkin in a large bowl and mash it with a fork – it can still be a bit lumpy, or you can mash until smooth if preferred. Add the ricotta, egg, quinoa, peas and chilli (if using) and stir gently to combine.

3. Line a baking tray with baking paper. Heat the remaining oil in a large non-stick frying pan over a medium heat. Take heaped tablespoonfuls of the mixture, place them in the pan and flatten them so they are 1–2 cm (½–¾ in) thick. Cook the fritters, in batches, for about 3 minutes on each side. Transfer the fritters to the prepared tray and finish cooking them in the oven for 5 minutes. Serve with the sweet chilli sauce, if desired.

Recipe image on page 23

Note

These fritters are also good the next day in lunchboxes, as an after-school snack or as a great alternative to a sandwich for a picnic.

Quinoa and
vegetable fritters
(page 25)

Vegetable and
haloumi fritters
(page 20)

Ricotta and
pumpkin fritters
(page 21)

Crunchy quinoa and vegetable fritters with lemon and herb mayonnaise

Quinoa is gluten free (although be aware there is also flour in this recipe) and high in protein and it gives these fritters (savoury pancakes) a delicious crunchy texture. Make the first couple of batches, then leave the last couple of batches to finish cooking in the oven while you sit down and enjoy the first lot! If you want a more substantial meal, serve some cucumber batons and cherry tomatoes on the side.

100 g (3½ oz/½ cup) quinoa
1 corn cob, husk and silk removed, or 150 g (5½ oz/ 1 cup) frozen corn kernels, defrosted
2 medium zucchini (courgettes), finely grated
2 medium carrots, peeled and coarsely grated
2 tablespoons finely chopped flat-leaf (Italian) parsley (optional)
3 eggs, lightly beaten
125 g (4½ oz) plain (all-purpose) flour
olive oil

Lemon and herb mayonnaise (optional)

90 g (3 oz/⅓ cup) good-quality whole egg mayonnaise
1 tablespoon finely chopped flat-leaf (Italian) parsley
2 teaspoons lemon juice
pinch of sea salt

1   Bring 250 ml (8½ fl oz/1 cup) of water to the boil in a medium saucepan. Add the quinoa, cover with a lid, reduce the heat and simmer for 15 minutes, or until all the water has been absorbed. Remove the pan from the heat, place a clean tea towel (dish towel) over the pan, cover with the lid and leave the quinoa for 5–10 minutes to absorb the remaining steam. Then cool.

2   Heat the oven to 200°C (400°F)/180°C (350°F) fan-forced and line a baking tray with baking paper. If you are making the lemon and herb mayonnaise, combine the ingredients in a small serving dish while the quinoa is cooking.

3   If you are using a corn cob, lie it on a board, then slice the kernels off each side using a sharp knife. Put the corn kernels in a bowl. Gently squeeze the liquid out of the zucchini and carrot in a tea towel (dish towel) or using clean hands, then add it to the corn along with the parsley (if using). Mix to combine.

4   Add the cooled quinoa and mix again. Add the egg and flour and season well with salt and pepper to taste. Mix to combine.

5   Add sufficient oil to just cover the base of a large non-stick frying pan and heat over a medium–high heat. Put heaped tablespoons of the batter into the pan and press down gently with the spoon to flatten slightly. Cook the fritters for 3 minutes until the base is golden. Turn over and cook for a further 2 minutes, then transfer to the lined tray. Finish cooking the fritters in the oven for 5 minutes.

6   Serve the fritters accompanied by the mayonnaise, if desired, or just plain mayonnaise.

San choy bao

San choy bao is a delicious Chinese dish, which is great to serve to kids – they can eat it with their hands, so no more arguments about holding cutlery properly for this meal! You can make it with either minced pork or chicken. There are many different versions of san choy bao, but I've kept mine as child-friendly as possible, with some optional extras for adults.

1 baby cos (romaine) lettuce
2 tablespoons soy sauce
2 tablespoons oyster sauce
1 teaspoon sesame oil
1 tablespoon vegetable oil
600 g (1 lb 5 oz) minced
  (ground) pork or chicken,
  preferably free-range
2 garlic cloves, crushed
½–1 red chilli, seeded and
  finely chopped (optional)
5 cm (2 in) piece of fresh
  ginger, finely grated
2 teaspoons white or
  brown sugar
1 large carrot, peeled and cut
  into matchsticks about 5 cm
  (2 in) long
75 g (2¾ oz) bean sprouts,
  trimmed
small handful of coriander
  (cilantro) leaves (optional)
lime wedges, to serve
  (optional)

1 Separate the lettuce leaves, then rinse and pat them dry. Place them on a plate and chill in the refrigerator until needed to keep them crisp.

2 In a small bowl, combine the soy sauce, oyster sauce and sesame oil.

3 Heat the vegetable oil in a wok or large frying pan, then add the meat and garlic and stir-fry for 1–2 minutes until the meat just changes colour – if you are using chicken, cook it for an extra minute.

4 Stir in the chilli (if using), the ginger and sugar, followed by the soy sauce mixture. Stir-fry for 2–3 minutes, or until the meat is cooked through.

5 Divide the mixture between the lettuce leaves and top with the carrot, bean sprouts and coriander leaves (if using). Alternatively, place all the ingredients on the table and get each person to build their own san choy bao. Serve immediately, with lime wedges if desired, and with lots of serviettes (napkins) – the dish can be messy to eat.

Warming vegetable and bean soup with pesto

For some kids, puréed soup can be challenging, so I don't purée this soup. I've added beans to make it a complete meal. I like to serve the soup with garlic bread – I've found that serving it with the bread encourages the kids to eat the soup because what they really want is the garlic bread! But this is optional, of course.

1 tablespoon olive oil
3 rashers (about 75 g/2¾ oz) of bacon, cut into 1 cm (½ in) cubes
1 onion, roughly chopped
1 garlic clove, crushed (optional)
2 medium carrots, peeled and chopped into 1 cm (½ in) pieces
2 zucchini (courgettes), chopped into 1 cm (½ in) pieces
1 litre (34 fl oz/4 cups) vegetable or chicken stock
400 g (14 oz) tinned diced tomatoes
400 g (14 oz) tinned beans, such as butter, borlotti or cannellini, drained and rinsed
150 g (5½ oz) frozen peas
60 g (2 oz/¼ cup) shop-bought pesto (or see recipes on page 64)

Garlic baguette (optional)

50 g (1¾ oz) butter
1 garlic clove, crushed
1 baguette (about 40 cm/ 1 ft 4 in long)

1 If you are making the garlic bread, prepare it first. Preheat the oven to 200°C (400°F)/180°C (350°F) fan-forced. Soften the butter to a spreadable consistency and stir in the garlic, then season with salt and pepper, if liked. Slice the baguette at 2–3 cm (¾–1¼ in) intervals, slicing about three-quarters of the way through. Carefully open out the slits and spread both sides with the garlic butter. Wrap in foil and set aside.

2 Heat the oil in a large saucepan over a medium heat and cook the bacon for 2 minutes. Add the onion, garlic (if using), carrot and zucchini and cook for 8–10 minutes until softened. Season with salt and pepper.

3 Add the stock and tomatoes, bring to the boil then reduce the heat and simmer for 5 minutes. If you are making garlic bread, put it in the oven now and bake for 10 minutes.

4 Add the beans to the saucepan, cover and cook for 5 minutes. Add the peas, return to the boil and cook for a further 2 minutes.

5 Divide the soup between bowls and serve with a dollop of pesto, or let everyone add their own pesto. Serve accompanied by the garlic bread for dunking.

Variation

You can also add pasta to this soup, either in place of or as well as the beans. Add about 200 g (7 oz) small pasta shapes (preferably wholemeal [whole-wheat]) to the soup in step 4 and cook for 10–15 minutes, or until the pasta is just cooked.

Note

To make this soup vegetarian, simply omit the bacon. And to make it vegan, remove the pesto, or use the Dairy-free pesto on page 64.

4 people ⏱ 20 minutes 🍳 5–12 minutes (depending if you are cooking meat)

Couscous salad with grilled haloumi

Eating a vegetarian meal a couple of times a week is good for the environment and for your family's health. However, if you do want to add some meat to this salad, I've included a recipe for a quick Moroccan lamb or chicken. Encouraging kids to eat couscous from an early age gives your family another option, rather than the usual rice, pasta or potatoes. Leftover couscous is perfect for lunch the next day.

Moroccan lamb or chicken (optional; see opposite page)
200 g (7 oz) couscous
250 ml (8½ fl oz/1 cup) boiling water
pinch of salt
1 lemon
2 tablespoons olive oil, plus extra for the haloumi
250 g (9 oz) cherry tomatoes, quartered
2 tablespoons finely chopped flat-leaf (Italian) parsley (optional)
2 medium carrots, peeled and coarsely grated
60 g (2 oz) rocket (arugula) or your choice of salad (optional)
500 g (1 lb 2 oz) haloumi

1 If you are adding lamb or chicken, prepare the meat first (see opposite page) and start cooking it once the couscous is soaking. Put the couscous in a large heatproof bowl and add the boiling water and salt. Stir, cover the bowl with a plate and leave the couscous to swell for 5 minutes. While the couscous is soaking, squeeze the juice from half the lemon and cut the remaining half into wedges.

2 Fluff up the couscous with a fork, ensuring you break up any lumps, then add the olive oil and 1 tablespoon of lemon juice. Stir gently to combine, then stir in the tomatoes, parsley (if using), carrot (see note) and rocket (if using). Season to taste with salt and pepper.

3 Slice the haloumi into fingers about 1 cm (½ in) thick and brush with oil. If you prepared either of the meat options, wipe out the pan the meat was cooked in and use it to fry the haloumi; otherwise, heat up a small amount of olive oil in a frying pan. Cook the haloumi for 1–2 minutes on each side, or until light golden.

4 Divide the couscous between plates and top with the haloumi and Moroccan lamb or chicken, if desired. Serve the lemon wedges for squeezing over.

Note

If you think your family won't like the couscous with all the vegetables mixed up in it, you can serve the carrots, cherry tomatoes, rocket (arugula) and parsley separately. Add the oil, lemon juice and seasoning to the couscous; just serve the other ingredients alongside.

Moroccan lamb or chicken

1 tablespoon olive oil
1 teaspoon ground cumin
1 teaspoon ground coriander
½ teaspoon smoked paprika
600 g (1 lb 5 oz) lamb fillet
  (backstrap), lamb cutlets or
  other quick-cooking cut, or
  600 g (1 lb 5 oz) boneless,
  skinless chicken breast,
  preferably free-range

1 Combine the oil and spices in a shallow dish and season with salt and pepper. Add the meat and turn to coat. Set aside for 10 minutes.

2 Heat a chargrill pan or frying pan over a high heat and cook the lamb for 2–3 minutes on each side, until cooked medium–rare, or to your liking. If you are using chicken, cook for 5–6 minutes on each side.

Variation

Instead of pasta you can use quinoa.
Simmer 200 g (7 oz/1 cup) of quinoa
in 375 ml (12½ fl oz/1½ cups) of water
for 15 minutes. Remove the pan from
the heat, place a clean tea towel
(dish towel) over the pan, cover with the
lid of the saucepan and let the quinoa
sit for 5–10 minutes to absorb any
remaining steam.

Maple-roasted pumpkin, chicken and pasta salad

I've talked about 'separatist' kids in my introduction and, as a parent of one (who fortunately has now grown out of it), I know that encouraging kids to eat salads from a young age is a good way to get them to try different flavours and textures. You can easily serve salads as individual components for the separatists (and this one is no exception) and tossed together for everyone else. When the separatists see the rest of the family eating the food all mixed up, hopefully one day they will too.

500 g (1 lb 2 oz) pumpkin (squash), such as butternut, kent or jap
½ teaspoon ground cinnamon (optional)
1 teaspoon ground cumin (optional)
1 teaspoon ground coriander (optional)
3 tablespoons olive oil
2 tablespoons maple syrup
600 g (1 lb 5 oz) boneless, skinless chicken breast, preferably free-range
1 teaspoon wholegrain mustard
300 g (10½ oz) wholemeal (whole-wheat) penne
2 corn cobs, husk and silk removed, or 250 g (9 oz) frozen corn kernels, defrosted
60 g (2 oz) rocket (arugula), or other salad leaf such as baby cos (romaine) lettuce

Dressing
2 tablespoons olive oil
2 teaspoons balsamic vinegar
1 teaspoon honey

1 Preheat the oven to 220°C (430°F)/200°C (400°F) fan-forced and line a baking tray with baking paper. Peel the pumpkin, cut it into 1 cm (½ in) cubes and place it on the tray. In a small bowl, combine the spices (if using), 1 tablespoon of the olive oil and 1 tablespoon of the maple syrup, then drizzle the mixture over the pumpkin. Season with salt and toss to coat. Roast the pumpkin in the oven for 15–20 minutes until tender. Remove from the oven and set aside to cool slightly.

2 Bring a large saucepan of salted water to the boil for the pasta. Cut the chicken breast horizontally into two thinner steaks: place your hand flat on top of the chicken and use a sharp knife to slice through, horizontally. In a shallow dish, combine 1 tablespoon of the olive oil, the remaining maple syrup and the mustard. Season with salt and pepper. Add the chicken and turn to coat.

3 Cook the penne in the boiling water according to the packet instructions, adding the corn cobs for the final 4 minutes of cooking (if using defrosted frozen corn kernels, add them for the final 2 minutes). Drain the pasta, but reserve 1 tablespoon of the cooking water.

4 While the pasta is cooking, heat the remaining tablespoon of olive oil in a large frying pan over a medium–high heat. Cook the chicken, in batches, for 3–4 minutes on each side until cooked through.

5 Coarsely tear any larger rocket or salad leaves into bite-sized pieces. Lie the corn cob on a board, then slice the kernels off each side using a sharp knife.

6 In a large bowl, combine the dressing ingredients with the pasta cooking water, season with salt and pepper and whisk to combine. Add the pasta, pumpkin, corn kernels and rocket to the dressing and toss gently. Tear or slice the chicken into bite-sized pieces, or thinly slice it, and either toss it through the salad or serve separately.

4 people　　 20 minutes　　🗄 20 minutes

Crunchy vegetable gado gado salad

Gado gado is an all-time favourite Indonesian dish with many families. A salad with crunchy carrots and cucumbers is simply delicious with the peanut sauce drizzled over. If you like a spicy sauce, add the chilli; otherwise, leave it out.

Gado gado sauce

1 lime
2 teaspoons vegetable oil
1 small garlic clove, crushed
170 ml (5½ fl oz) tinned
  coconut milk
70 g (2½ oz/¼ cup) peanut
  butter (smooth or crunchy)
2 teaspoons soy sauce
½–1 red chilli, seeded and
  finely chopped (optional)
20 g (¾ oz) peanuts,
  roughly chopped

Vegetable salad

8 small waxy potatoes, such
  as new potatoes, halved
150 g (5½ oz) green beans,
  ends trimmed, halved
4 eggs
1–2 tablespoons vegetable oil
200 g (7 oz) firm tofu, cut into
  triangles (optional)
2 Lebanese (short)
  cucumbers, thickly sliced
2 firm, ripe tomatoes,
  cut into wedges
2 medium carrots, peeled,
  halved and cut into thin
  matchsticks
large handful of bean sprouts,
  ends trimmed

1 For the gado gado sauce, finely grate the zest from half the lime, then squeeze the juice from the same half. Cut the remaining half into wedges.

2 Heat the oil in a small saucepan over a medium–low heat. Cook the garlic for 30 seconds, then add the coconut milk, lime zest and peanut butter and stir until combined. Simmer for 2–3 minutes until heated through. Remove the pan from the heat and stir in the soy sauce, chilli (if using) and 2 teaspoons of the lime juice. Set aside. The sauce can be served hot or cold – it is best served cold with this salad.

3 For the vegetable salad, put the potatoes in a medium saucepan of salted water and bring to the boil. Next, bring a small saucepan of water to the boil. Simmer the potatoes for 15 minutes, adding the green beans for the final 2–3 minutes, until the beans and potatoes are tender. Drain the beans and potatoes and refresh under cold water. Cut the potatoes into thin wedges.

4 Meanwhile, boil the eggs in the small saucepan of water for 7 minutes. Drain and refresh under cold water. Peel, then cut into wedges.

5 If you are using the tofu, heat 1 tablespoon of the oil in a large frying pan over a medium heat and fry the tofu for 2–3 minutes on each side, until lightly golden. Drain on paper towel.

6 Heat the remaining tablespoon of oil in the pan, add the potatoes and fry for 2–3 minutes until golden. Drain on paper towel.

7 To serve, arrange the potatoes, beans, cucumber, tomato, carrot, tofu and eggs on a platter. Stir the chopped peanuts through the gado gado sauce, then drizzle the sauce over the salad or serve it separately on the side. Scatter over the bean sprouts and serve.

Quinoa and rice salad with bocconcini or haloumi

You can also use brown rice for this salad, and if you'd rather do this, cook the rice according to the packet instructions (separate from the quinoa) and then add it to the salad. The addition of quinoa makes this recipe healthier than a normal rice salad and introduces new flavours to kids. Basmati rice has a lower GI then jasmine, but if you only have jasmine it's fine to use that instead.

1 red capsicum (bell pepper), core and seeds removed, cut into 1 cm (½ in) cubes

1 small eggplant (aubergine), about 200–300 g/7–10½ oz, cut into 1 cm (½ in) cubes

1 teaspoon ground cumin

1 teaspoon ground coriander

3 tablespoons olive oil, plus 2 teaspoons extra if using haloumi

100 g (3½ oz/½ cup) quinoa

95 g (3½ oz/½ cup) basmati rice

pinch of sea salt

2 handfuls of baby English spinach leaves

250 g (9 oz) cherry or grape tomatoes, quartered, or 3 medium tomatoes, diced

180 g (6½ oz) tub of bocconcini (baby mozzarella), halved, or 250 g (9 oz) haloumi, thinly sliced

1 Preheat the oven to 200°C (400°F)/180°C (350°F) fan-forced and line a baking tray with baking paper. Place the capsicum and eggplant on the tray. Sprinkle over the ground cumin and coriander and drizzle with 2 tablespoons of the olive oil. Toss to coat. Roast for 20 minutes, or until the eggplant is very soft (no one likes spongy eggplant).

2 Meanwhile, bring 375 ml (12½ fl oz/1½ cups) of water to the boil in a medium saucepan. Rinse the quinoa and rice well, then add them to the water with the salt. Cover with a lid and simmer gently for 12–15 minutes, or until the water has been absorbed. Remove from the heat, place a tea towel (dish towel) over the pan, cover with the lid and leave the quinoa and rice to stand for 5–10 minutes to absorb the remaining steam.

3 Put the rice and quinoa in a large bowl and add the capsicum and eggplant. Add the baby spinach and toss to wilt it slightly, then stir in the tomato and 1 tablespoon of oil. Check the seasoning and adjust if necessary.

4 If you are using bocconcini, stir it through the salad. If you are using haloumi, heat 2 teaspoons of oil in a frying pan over a medium–high heat and fry the haloumi on both sides for 1–2 minutes until light golden. Arrange the haloumi on top of the salad. The salad can be served warm or at room temperature. However, if using haloumi, I would suggest serving the haloumi hot.

Note

Leftover rice or quinoa is great for lunch or dinner the next day. Simply add crumbled feta or goat's cheese, diced cucumber and tomato, avocado and a handful of fresh herbs (flat-leaf [Italian] parsley or coriander [cilantro]). Serve with a squeeze of lemon or a splash of white-wine, red-wine or apple-cider vinegar and a dash of olive oil.

4 people   20 minutes   7 minutes

Fragrant Thai noodle salad

This is a great salad to start introducing different flavours to kids from a young age. Place the optional flavourings on the table and encourage everyone to add bits to their own dish. In a Thai salad like this, the herbs are an integral part of the flavour and not just for garnish, so as your family starts to like the flavour of fresh herbs, add more.

1 or more of the protein options (see box)
200 g (7 oz) vermicelli noodles
juice of 2 limes
1 tablespoon vegetable oil
2 tablespoons fish sauce
1½ teaspoons brown or white sugar
1 teaspoon soy sauce
250 g (9 oz) cherry, grape or baby roma (plum) tomatoes, quartered, or 3 medium firm, ripe tomatoes, diced
2 Lebanese (short) cucumbers
150 g (5½ oz) snow peas (mangetout), raw or blanched, ends trimmed, thinly sliced lengthways
1 long red chilli, seeded and thinly sliced (optional)
small handful of mint leaves (optional)
small handful of coriander (cilantro) leaves (optional)

1 Prepare your choice of protein. Meanwhile, put the noodles in a heatproof bowl and cover with boiling water. Leave to soften for 6–7 minutes (or according to the packet instructions for a salad), then drain. Rinse under warm running water to prevent the noodles sticking together. Drain the noodles well, then put them in a large serving bowl. Using scissors, cut them into shorter lengths.

2 While the noodles are softening, combine 2 tablespoons of the lime juice with the oil, fish sauce, sugar and soy sauce in a small bowl, adjusting the taste to suit – you can add a little more lime juice, sugar or fish sauce to balance the flavour of sour, sweet and salty. Pour half of the dressing over the noodles and toss well to combine.

3 Add the tomatoes to the noodles. Cut the cucumbers in half lengthways, scoop out the seeds with a teaspoon, then dice the flesh. Add the cucumber and snow peas to the noodles.

4 Add the chilli and herbs (if using), or serve them separately in bowls for each family member to add their own. Add your choice of protein to the salad, drizzle with the remaining dressing and serve.

Recipe image on pages 40 & 41

Protein options

Pretty much any protein will work with this salad. You could even use leftover roast chicken or beef, or cooked salmon fillet. Make the salad, then either serve the protein on top or toss it through the salad just before serving.

Chicken: Put 600 g (1 lb 5 oz) boneless, skinless chicken breast (preferably free-range) in a medium saucepan and just cover with water. Cover with a lid and bring to a simmer. Simmer for 5 minutes, then remove the pan from the heat and leave the chicken to finish poaching for 15 minutes. Drain the chicken, then shred it. Alternatively, chargrill the chicken until cooked through, then slice it. Add the chicken to the salad.

Prawns: Peel and devein 600 g (1 lb 5 oz) raw medium king prawns (jumbo shrimp), or use 500 g (1 lb 2 oz) raw peeled prawns. Cook the prawns in simmering water for 3–4 minutes, or until they turn bright pink. Drain and refresh the prawns under cold water, then add them to the salad. Or buy 500 g (1 lb 2 oz) cooked, peeled prawns and add them straight to the salad.

Tofu: Cut 600 g (1 lb 5 oz) firm tofu into 1 cm (½ in) cubes. Pan-fry it in 1–2 tablespoons of vegetable oil for 3–4 minutes, turning regularly until golden, then add it to the salad.

Beef: Brush about 600 g (1 lb 5 oz) beef steak, such as fillet (tenderloin) or sirloin, with oil and season with salt and pepper. Cook in a hot chargrill pan for 2–3 minutes on each side (depending on the thickness of the steak), until cooked to your liking. Rest for 3 minutes, then slice the meat thinly and add it to the salad.

'Pulled' chicken in tortilla wraps

These tortilla wraps aren't as packed full of vegetables as most of my recipes, so when I make them I hand every member of the family (yes, including my husband) a large raw carrot to snack on while I make dinner! This dish is pretty quick to put together and then it just does its own thing in the oven for about an hour. It's a one-pot meal, so there isn't much washing up either – bonus!

600–800 g (1 lb 5 oz–1 lb 12 oz) boneless, skinless chicken thighs, preferably free-range (or breast – but cook for 45 minutes only)
1–2 tablespoons olive oil
1 teaspoon ground cumin
1 teaspoon ground coriander
½ teaspoon smoked paprika
1 tablespoon balsamic vinegar (or red-wine, white-wine or apple-cider vinegar)
400 g (14 oz) tinned crushed tomatoes
1 teaspoon finely chopped chipotle chilli in adobo sauce (optional; see note on page 94)
10 × 20 cm (8 in) flour tortillas
400 g (14 oz) tinned black beans, drained and rinsed
2 tablespoons coarsely chopped coriander (cilantro) (optional)
approximately 150 g (5½ oz) sour cream
1 large avocado, thinly sliced

1 Preheat the oven to 170°C (340°F)/160°C (320°F) fan-forced. Cut each piece of chicken in half and season with salt and pepper to taste. Heat 1 tablespoon of the oil in a large flameproof casserole dish over a medium–high heat and fry the chicken, in batches if necessary, for 2–3 minutes on each side, or until light golden. Add more oil to the pan if required. Remove from the pan.

2 Reduce the heat to medium–low and add the ground cumin, coriander and paprika and cook for 30 seconds, stirring to prevent the spices burning. Add the vinegar and, using a wooden spoon, dislodge the crusty bits from the base of the pan. Add the tomatoes and chilli (if using), season with salt and pepper and bring to the boil.

3 Return the chicken and any resting juices to the pan, pushing it down to ensure it is submerged. Cover with a lid and cook in the oven for 1 hour.

4 Warm the tortillas according to the packet instructions. If warming them in the oven, put them in 5 minutes before the hour of cooking is up.

5 Remove the chicken from the oven. Using two forks, shred the chicken into the sauce, which should be quite thick by now. Stir in the beans and return the chicken to the oven for 5 minutes with the lid off to thicken the sauce.

6 Take the chicken out of the oven and stir in the fresh coriander (if using), or leave it out and add it later just for those who like it. Either place all the components on the table for everyone to make their own wraps, or assemble them before serving. Spread each tortilla with sour cream, then top with some of the chicken mix. Top with avocado and any remaining coriander (if using). Tuck up the bottom and roll up to enclose the wrap. These are best eaten with a knife and fork as they can get messy.

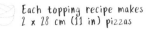
Pizzas for the whole family

Please welcome into your pizza-making life the humble Lebanese pitta bread! These breads make a great substitute base, particularly if you like your pizza thin and crispy, and they are generally far healthier than supermarket bases. I've suggested a few different topping ideas, including some additions that may appeal more to the adults. If you prefer to make your own bases, that's fine too – just use the topping ideas.

Red capsicum, pesto and cherry tomato pizza

1 tablespoon olive oil
1 red capsicum (bell pepper),
  core and seeds removed,
  thinly sliced
3 tablespoons Basil pesto (see
  page 64)
1 garlic clove, crushed
80 ml (2½ fl oz/⅓ cup)
  tomato passata (puréed
  tomatoes)
2 × 28 cm (11 in) pitta breads
  (wholemeal/whole-wheat
  or white)
300 g (10½ oz/2 cups)
  coarsely grated mozzarella
250 g (9 oz) cherry tomatoes,
  halved
small handful of basil leaves

1 Preheat the oven to 220°C (430°F)/200°C (400°F) fan-forced. Line two baking trays with baking paper.

2 Heat the olive oil in a medium frying pan over a medium-high heat and cook the capsicum for 4–5 minutes, until softened and slightly blackened. Remove the pan from the heat and stir in the pesto.

3 Stir the garlic into the passata and season with salt and pepper to taste. Place a pitta bread on each prepared tray and spread each bread with the passata. Top with the cheese almost to the edge, then top with the cherry tomatoes and capsicum.

4 Bake for 8–10 minutes until the cheese has melted and the bases are crisp around the edges. You may have to switch them around in the oven (top to bottom) to ensure they cook evenly. Just before serving, scatter the pizzas with basil leaves.

Recipe image on page 45
More pizza recipes on pages 46 & 47

Multi-coloured vegetable pizza (page 47)

Double cheese, ham and rocket pizza (page 46)

Red capsicum, pesto and cherry tomato pizza (page 43)

Double cheese, ham and rocket pizza

1 garlic clove, crushed
80 ml (2½ fl oz)
tomato passata (puréed
   tomatoes)
2 × 28 cm (11 in) pitta breads
   (wholemeal/whole-wheat
   or white)
300 g (10½ oz/2 cups)
   coarsely grated mozzarella
100 g (3½ oz) ham off the
   bone, roughly chopped
   180 g (6½ oz) bocconcini
   (baby mozzarella), halved, or
   mozzarella, diced
20 pitted kalamata olives,
   halved (optional)
50 g (1¾ oz) rocket (arugula)
   leaves

1 Preheat the oven to 220°C (430°F)/200°C (400°F) fan-forced. Line two baking trays with baking paper.

2 Stir the garlic into the passata and season with salt and pepper to taste. Place a pitta bread on each prepared tray. Spread each bread with the passata. Top with the grated mozzarella almost to the edge, then top with the ham and bocconcini. Scatter over the olives (if using).

3 Bake for 8–10 minutes until the cheese has melted and the bases are crisp around the edges. You may have to switch them around in the oven (top to bottom) to ensure they cook evenly. Just before serving, scatter the pizzas with rocket.

Recipe image on page 44

Multi-coloured vegetable pizza

You can change the vegetables to suit your family, but putting colourful vegetables on pizza will hopefully inspire them to eat them. If you catch your kids young enough, maybe they will think pizzas are always covered in vegetables! I was amazed at how much everyone (well nearly everyone – see the small aside below) loved this colourful pizza.

1 corn cob, husk and silk removed, or 200 g (7 oz/ 1⅓ cups) frozen corn kernels, defrosted

150 g (5½ oz) broccoli, cut into very small florets

2 × 28 cm (11 in) pitta breads (wholemeal/whole-wheat or white)

80 ml (2½ fl oz/⅓ cup) tomato passata (puréed tomatoes)

300 g (10½ oz/2 cups) coarsely grated mozzarella

250 g (9 oz) cherry tomatoes, quartered

1 orange or yellow capsicum (bell pepper), core and seeds removed, thinly sliced

small handful of basil leaves (optional)

1 Preheat the oven to 220°C (430°F)/200°C (400°F) fan-forced. If you are using a corn cob, cook it in a saucepan of boiling salted water for 2 minutes, then remove it from the pan using tongs. Return the water to the boil and cook the broccoli florets for 2–3 minutes until tender. Drain well and set aside in a colander. Lie the corn cob on a board, then slice the kernels off each side using a sharp knife.

2 Line two baking trays with baking paper and place a pitta bread on each prepared tray. Spread each bread with the passata. Top with the cheese, almost to the edge. Arrange the broccoli, corn kernels, tomatoes and capsicum in circles on the bases.

3 Bake for 8–10 minutes until the cheese has melted and the bases are crisp around the edges. You may have to switch them around in the oven (top to bottom) to ensure they cook evenly. Just before serving, scatter the pizzas with basil leaves (if using).

Recipe image on page 44

A small aside ...

Don't let you kids read this, but forevermore, the Multi-coloured vegetable pizza will be known as 'Disappointment pizza' by my family! My youngest son was very excited when I said we were having pizza for dinner, but when he saw it had broccoli on it, his grumpy response was, 'well, I'll just call it disappointment pizza'. However, you'll be glad to know that the whole thing was eaten and enjoyed by everyone, and has since made a regular appearance.

NOODLES, PASTA & RICE

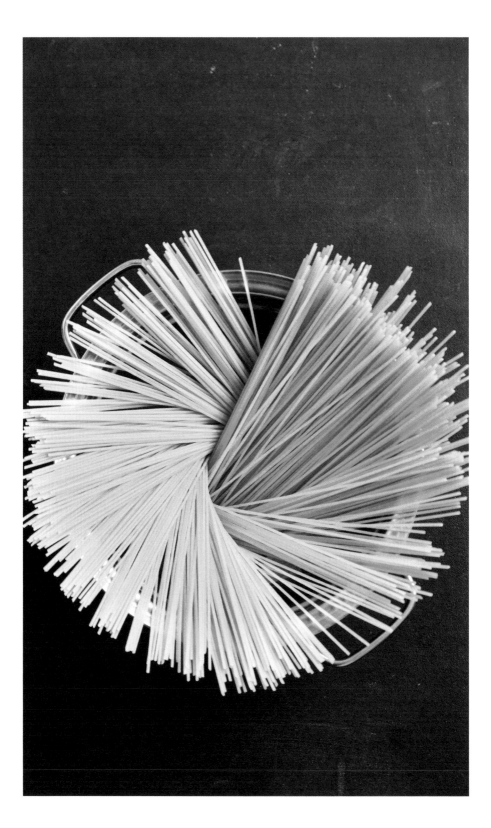

In this chapter, you'll find a great selection of recipes from all around the world — Asian noodle soup and stir-fries, Italian pastas, risotto, curry and a Cajun-inspired rice dish. Hopefully, some of these will become your family's favourites in no time.

Aromatic chicken noodle soup

This dish might seem like hard work, but it really isn't. Plus, unless you have a very hungry family, you will end up with some delicious poached chicken leftovers for lunches the next day. I make this about once a week, especially when I'm working from home – or at the weekend, when I'm around to check the saucepan gently simmering away.

You may not want to start this soup from scratch at the end of a long day at work, so steps 1 and 2 can be completed the day before and kept in the refrigerator, then the soup is far quicker to assemble the next day.

1 tablespoon vegetable oil

2–3 teaspoons finely grated fresh ginger

270 g (9½ oz) dried ramen or soba noodles, or spaghetti

1 tablespoon kecap manis (see note)

1 tablespoon fish sauce

3 teaspoons soy sauce

200 g (7 oz) snow peas (mangetout), ends trimmed, thinly sliced lengthways

3 medium carrots, peeled, halved and cut into thin matchsticks

small handful of coriander (cilantro) leaves or Vietnamese mint (optional)

1 long red chilli, thinly sliced (optional)

Soup base

1 small onion, roughly chopped

1 medium carrot, peeled and roughly chopped

1 corn cob, husk and silk removed, or 150 g (5½ oz/1 cup) frozen corn kernels, defrosted

2 star anise

4 thin slices of fresh ginger

2–3 coriander (cilantro) stalks (optional)

1 whole chicken, preferably free-range, about 1.4 kg (3 lb 1 oz)

1 For the soup base, put the onion and carrot in a large stockpot or saucepan with the corn cob (if using frozen corn kernels, do not add them at this stage), star anise, ginger and coriander stalks (if using). Remove any excess fat from around the neck opening of the chicken, then add the chicken to the pan. Cover with 1.6–1.8 litres (54–61 fl oz) of water and put the lid on. Bring it slowly to the boil, skimming off any scum that rises to the surface. Reduce the heat to low and simmer, covered, for 1 hour.

2 Carefully remove the chicken from the stockpot (this is probably easiest done using tongs) and put it in a large bowl. Strain the soup into another large saucepan or a very large jug, reserving the corn cob and star anise and discarding the remaining flavourings. (At this stage the soup stock can be stored in the refrigerator until using. Remove any fat from the surface once cold.)

3 Rinse out the pan. Heat the vegetable oil in the stockpot over a medium heat. Add the grated ginger and reserved star anise and stir-fry for 1 minute. Add the reserved soup and bring to the boil. Simmer hard for about 10 minutes to reduce the liquid slightly and intensify the flavour of the stock.

4 Bring a medium saucepan of water to the boil for the noodles. Lie the corn cob on a board, then slice the kernels off each side using a sharp knife.

5 Remove the skin from the chicken and shred the meat – the meat should just fall off the bones.

6 Cook the noodles for 4 minutes in the boiling water, or according to the packet instructions. Drain and rinse under hot water and set aside.

7 Stir the kecap manis, fish sauce and soy sauce into the soup. Add the snow peas and carrot and cook for 2 minutes. Add the corn kernels and cook for a further 1–2 minutes, until the vegetables are tender.

8 Divide the noodles between deep bowls and top with some shredded chicken. Ladle over the soup and vegetables and serve topped with the coriander and red chilli (if using) for those who like them. Eat with a combination of spoon and fork, or chopsticks and spoon, and provide serviettes for wiping the soup off your chins!

Note

Kecap manis is an Indonesian sweet soy sauce, available from many supermarkets or Asian stores. It's delicious added to stir-fries as well.

Teriyaki salmon with udon noodles and stir-fried vegetables

The teriyaki salmon part of this meal is another of my 'go-to' dinners, and makes a regular appearance when we go camping. It's also a great dish to keep in the freezer – marinate the fish to be frozen in a freezer bag for 2–3 hours in the refrigerator, then freeze it. Defrost it in the refrigerator before cooking. The stir-fried vegetables are fairly simple because the teriyaki salmon is very flavoursome.

Teriyaki salmon
60 ml (2 fl oz/¼ cup) soy
    sauce
2 tablespoons mirin
2 teaspoons caster (superfine)
    sugar
1 tablespoon honey
600–800 g (1 lb 5 oz–1 lb 12 oz)
    skinless salmon fillet

Stir-fried vegetables and noodles
1 bunch baby bok choy (pak
    choy) (see variations on
    page 56)
270 g (9½ oz) dried udon
    noodles
1 teaspoon sesame oil
1 tablespoon vegetable oil
1 garlic clove, crushed
2 teaspoons finely grated
    fresh ginger
150 g (5½ oz) snow peas
    (mangetout), ends trimmed,
    thinly sliced lengthways
small handful of coriander
    (cilantro) leaves (optional)

1 For the teriyaki salmon, combine the soy sauce, mirin, sugar and honey in a small saucepan. Bring to the boil, then simmer for 2 minutes. Pour the mixture into a shallow dish and leave to cool for 10 minutes. Set aside the saucepan to reuse later.

2 Meanwhile, cut the salmon into four portions and remove any remaining bones. Place the fish in the cooled marinade and turn to coat. Set aside for 10–15 minutes. Line a baking tray with foil and place a grill (broiler) shelf about 10 cm (4 in) away from the heat.

3 To prepare the noodles and vegetables, bring a large saucepan of water to the boil for the noodles. Next, trim the ends of the bok choy, then shred the stalks and leaves, keeping the stalks and leaves separate.

4 Cook the noodles in the boiling water for 10 minutes, or according to the packet instructions. Drain the noodles well and rinse them under hot water to prevent them from sticking. Return the noodles to the saucepan, add the sesame oil and toss to coat.

5 While the noodles are cooking, heat the grill to high. Remove the salmon from the marinade (reserving the marinade) and place it on the lined tray. Grill (broil) the salmon for 3–4 minutes on each side, or until the fish is just cooked through. The exact cooking time will depend on the thickness of your fish. Pour the reserved marinade back into the small saucepan and warm it through over a very low heat.

Continued on page 56

Note

Mirin is a sweet, spirit-based rice liquid available from some supermarkets and from Asian food stores. Along with soy, it is the traditional ingredient of teriyaki.

6   Once you turn the fish, heat 1 tablespoon of the vegetable oil in a wok or large frying pan over a medium heat. Add the garlic and ginger and stir-fry for 30 seconds, or until fragrant. Increase the heat to high, add the bok choy stalks and 1 tablespoon of water and stir-fry for 1 minute. Add the snow peas and bok choy leaves and stir-fry for 2 minutes, or until the vegetables are tender.

7   Divide the noodles between bowls and top with the stir-fried vegetables and a piece of salmon. Spoon over the hot marinade and scatter over coriander leaves (if using).

Variations

You can swap around the vegetables to suit your family. Green beans, red capsicum (bell pepper) and mushrooms all work well too. Carrots can be used, but slice them thinly and add 1–2 tablespoons of water to the pan to help them cook – they will take 3–4 minutes.

Chicken and vegetable stir-fry

Gado gado (see page 34) is usually served as a salad. However, I think it's the peanut sauce that everyone loves the most, so I've used it in this chicken and vegetable stir-fry. If you like a spicy sauce, add chilli; otherwise, leave it out.

1 quantity Gado gado sauce (see page 34)

300 g (10½ oz) fresh egg noodles, or 350 g (12½ oz) dried egg noodles

2 teaspoons sesame oil

2 tablespoons vegetable oil

600 g (1 lb 5 oz) boneless, skinless chicken breast, preferably free-range, cut into thin slices

2 medium carrots, peeled, halved lengthways, then cut into thin semi-circles

1 bunch baby bok choy (pak choy), ends trimmed, stalk and leaves thinly sliced

150 g (5½ oz) sugar snap peas or snow peas (mangetout), ends trimmed

1 tablespoon soy sauce

40 g (1½ oz/¼ cup) coarsely chopped peanuts

1 Prepare the gado gado sauce and set aside in a small saucepan.

2 Bring a large saucepan of water to the boil for the noodles. Cover the saucepan with a lid and keep at a simmer. If you are using fresh egg noodles, separate them and set aside.

3 Meanwhile, heat 1 tablespoon of the vegetable oil in a wok or large frying pan over a high heat. Add the chicken, in batches, and stir-fry for 2–3 minutes until light golden and cooked through. Set aside.

4 Heat the remaining tablespoon of vegetable oil in the pan. Add the carrot and 1 tablespoon of water and stir-fry for 2 minutes. Add the bok choy stalks and stir-fry for 1 minute.

5 Next, cook the noodles. Cook fresh noodles in boiling water for 2 minutes or according to the packet instructions, then drain well. Rinse the noodles under hot water to prevent them from sticking. Cook dried noodles according to the packet instructions, then drain and rinse as for the fresh noodles. Return the noodles to the saucepan and drizzle over the sesame oil. Toss to coat.

6 Add the sugar snap peas, bok choy leaves and soy sauce to the stir-fry and stir-fry for 1–2 minutes, or until all the vegetables are tender. Return the chicken to the pan and toss to combine. Warm up the gado gado sauce over a medium heat. Divide the noodles between bowls, top with the chicken and vegetable stir-fry and drizzle over the hot gado gado sauce. Scatter over the peanuts and serve.

Note

For speed, the onion and garlic can be left out. Sometimes I add them, sometimes I don't. They are there for a little extra flavour. Also, it's a great way to subtly introduce kids to the flavour of garlic.

Hidden gem meatballs with spaghetti and tomato sauce

These meatballs are one of the first answers I get from my kids to the 'What do you want for dinner tonight?' question. I don't mind one bit because they are full of vegetables (the 'hidden gem'). My kids had no idea for a long time – of course, now that they love them so much, it's far too late to complain about the vegetables!

3 tablespoons olive oil

1 onion, coarsely grated (see note)

2 garlic cloves, crushed or finely chopped

2 medium carrots, peeled and finely grated

2 zucchini (courgettes), about 250 g (9 oz) in total, finely grated

2 tablespoons finely chopped flat-leaf (Italian) parsley

1 teaspoon wholegrain mustard

600 g (1 lb 5 oz) lean minced (ground) beef

75 g (2¾ oz/1¼ cups) panko breadcrumbs

1 egg, lightly beaten

700 ml (23½ fl oz) tomato passata (puréed tomatoes)

350 g (12½ oz) spaghetti or other pasta shape

50 g (1¾ oz/½ cup) finely grated parmesan or tasty cheese

2 tablespoons coarsely torn basil leaves (optional)

1 Heat 1 tablespoon of the olive oil in a large frying pan over a medium heat. Cook the onion and garlic for 4–5 minutes, or until softened, then transfer them to a large bowl.

2 Using clean hands (or a clean tea towel/dish towel) squeeze out any excess liquid from the grated carrot and zucchini. Add them to the bowl along with the parsley, mustard, meat, panko breadcrumbs and egg. Season with salt and pepper (if liked). Using your hands, combine the mixture, mixing for a couple of minutes. Form the mixture into golf ball–sized meatballs. If you have time, chill them in the refrigerator for 10 minutes, but this is not vital.

3 Bring a large saucepan of salted water to the boil for the pasta. Heat the remaining oil in the frying pan over a medium heat and add the meatballs in a single layer (or do this in two batches if necessary, but return all the meatballs to the pan when adding the passata). Cook for 4–5 minutes, turning occasionally, until the meatballs start to brown. Add the passata to the pan and shake the pan. Using a wooden spoon, carefully scrape between the meatballs to dislodge any crusty bits from the base of the pan. Turn the meatballs to coat them in the sauce, then cover the pan with a lid, reduce the heat to low and simmer for 10–15 minutes, or until the meatballs are cooked through.

4 Cook the pasta according to the packet instructions. Drain, reserving 1 tablespoon of the cooking liquid.

5 Stir the reserved cooking liquid into the tomato sauce. Divide the spaghetti between bowls and top with the meatballs and sauce. Scatter over the cheese and basil (if using).

Variation

These meatballs can also be baked. Once they've had their initial browning, transfer them to an ovenproof dish. Spoon over the sauce and turn to coat, then scatter over the cheese and bake in a 190°C (375°F) oven/170°C (340°F) fan-forced for about 15 minutes.

Marinara pasta with napoletana sauce

It's important to encourage your family to eat fish. Here, mixed seafood is combined with a rich tomato sauce and served over pasta. The tomato sauce ensures the seafood flavour isn't overwhelming, so it should appeal to kids. You can use either a good-quality marinara mix (a mix of prepared fish and seafood) from your fishmonger or supermarket, or the equivalent amount of your family's favourite fish or seafood.

600–700 g (1 lb 5 oz–1 lb 9 oz) mixed seafood (see note)
1 tablespoon olive oil
1 onion, finely chopped
1 garlic clove, crushed or finely chopped
125 ml (4 fl oz/½ cup) white wine (optional)
800 g (1 lb 12 oz) tinned crushed or diced tomatoes
350 g (12½ oz) spaghetti
1 tablespoon coarsely chopped flat-leaf (Italian) parsley (optional)

1 If you are using mussels still in their shells, complete this step; otherwise, move on to step 2. Scrub the mussels, then pull off the hairy beards. Put 125 ml (4 fl oz/½ cup) of water in a large deep frying pan over a high heat and bring it to the boil. Add the mussels, pop the lid on and cook for 2–3 minutes, or until the shells open. Remove the mussels from the cooking liquid and carefully remove each mussel from its shell. (Discard any unopened mussels.) Reserve the cooking liquid.

2 Bring a large saucepan of water to the boil for the spaghetti. Heat the oil in a deep frying pan over a medium heat and cook the onion and garlic for 5 minutes. Add the white wine (if using), bring to the boil, then boil for 1 minute. Add the tomato, season with salt and pepper and bring to a simmer. Simmer, uncovered, for 10 minutes. Cook the spaghetti according to the packet instructions.

3 Meanwhile, if you are using your own seafood mix, cut the fish fillets into 2 cm (¾ in) pieces. Cut any prawns in half, or leave them whole if preferred. Cut squid tubes into 1 cm (½ in) rings.

4 If you are using a marinara mix, add it to the sauce now and cook for 2–3 minutes, or until all the fish is just cooked through. If you are using your own mix, add the fish and prawns to the sauce and simmer for 2 minutes. Add any squid rings and simmer for a further 2 minutes. Stir in mussels just to heat them through.

5 If a stronger seafood flavour is liked, add the reserved mussel cooking liquid to the sauce (if available). Just before serving, stir in the parsley (if using), or scatter it over, and serve the sauce over the spaghetti.

Note

To create your own seafood mix, use 400 g (14 oz) skinless white fish (such as ling, flathead or cod), 8 raw, peeled, deveined prawns (shrimp), 8 black mussels and 2 squid tubes (or adapt to your family's taste). Salmon is also a great addition.

Vegetable and bocconcini pasta bake

This is another of my 'go-to' meals, where I add different things depending on what is in the refrigerator. I usually make it vegetarian, although I have provided meat options as well. Once this dish is in the oven you are free to go and listen to your child read, chat about their day or help with their homework.

350 g (12½ oz) penne or rigatoni (wholemeal/whole-wheat or regular)
3 tablespoons olive oil
1 medium eggplant (aubergine), cut into 1 cm (½ in) cubes
1 red capsicum (bell pepper), core and seeds removed, cut into 1 cm (½ in) cubes
1 garlic clove, crushed
700 ml (23½ fl oz) tomato passata (puréed tomatoes)
220 g (8 oz) bocconcini (baby mozzarella) or mozzarella, cut into 1–2 cm (½–¾ in) cubes
35 g (1¼ oz/⅓ cup) finely grated parmesan
crisp green salad, or rocket (arugula) salad, to serve (optional)
small handful of basil leaves to serve (optional)

1 Cook the pasta according to the packet instructions.

2 Meanwhile, heat the oven to 200°C (400°F)/180°C (350°F) fan-forced. Heat 2 tablespoons of the oil in a flameproof casserole dish over a medium–high heat. Add the eggplant and cook for 5–6 minutes until light golden and softened. Remove the eggplant from the pan.

3 Reduce the heat to medium, heat the remaining tablespoon of oil in the pan and fry the capsicum for 3 minutes. Add the garlic and cook for a further minute. Return the eggplant to the pan with the passata and bocconcini. Season with salt and pepper and stir to combine. Bring to a simmer, then cook for a couple of minutes until the cheese starts to melt.

4 Remove the pan from the heat and stir in the cooked pasta and half the parmesan. Stir to coat the pasta in the sauce. Scatter over the remaining parmesan, then transfer the casserole dish to the oven and bake, uncovered, for 20–25 minutes, or until the top is golden and bubbling.

5 Meanwhile, prepare your salad, if serving. Scatter the basil leaves over the pasta (if using) and serve.

Variations

If you would like to add some meat to this dish, either fry up 200 g (7 oz) diced bacon and stir it through the sauce before baking, or add 200 g (7 oz) diced good-quality ham to the sauce before baking. You could also slice up four sausages, fry them briefly, then add them to the sauce before baking. If your kids like mushrooms, these are also delicious fried off with the other vegetables.

4 people   30 minutes   12 minutes

Zoodles with chicken and pesto

Zucchini noodles or 'zoodles' are a great alternative to pasta, made by spiralising zucchini. I've included three different pesto recipes, including a dairy-free one, all of which can be used in multiple recipes. If you have kids who are adamant they don't like zucchini, why not peel the zucchini before making the zoodles so then they are white. This way it's highly unlikely they will realise they are zucchini – just a devious mum thought!

600 g (1 lb 5 oz) boneless, skinless chicken breast, preferably free-range
finely grated zest and juice of 1 lemon
80 ml (2½ fl oz/⅓ cup) olive oil
1 teaspoon dried oregano
5 medium zucchini (courgettes), about 500 g (1 lb 2 oz) in total (see note on page 65)
1 quantity pesto (see the recipes on page 64), or about 190 g (6½ oz) good-quality store-bought pesto
250 g (9 oz) cherry tomatoes, quartered
a few basil leaves to serve (optional)
carrot and/or cucumber batons to serve (optional)

1 Cut each chicken breast into two thinner steaks. To do this, place your hand flat on top of the chicken and use a sharp knife to slice through, horizontally.

2 Combine the lemon zest, 2 tablespoons of the olive oil and the oregano in a shallow dish and season with salt and pepper. Add the chicken and turn to coat. Set aside to marinate.

3 Trim the ends of the zucchini, then use a spiraliser to cut the zucchini into 'zoodles' (or see the note on page 65 on how to hand-cut them). Put the zoodles between layers of paper towel and pat them dry, pressing down firmly to remove any excess water. Set aside on paper towel.

4 If you are making your own pesto, prepare it now.

5 Heat a large frying pan over a medium–high heat and dry-fry the chicken, in batches if necessary, for 3–4 minutes on each side, or until cooked through. Transfer to a plate and pour over the lemon juice. Turn the chicken to coat. Set the chicken aside and keep it warm.

6 Wipe out the pan and heat 1 tablespoon of olive oil in the same pan over a high heat. Once the oil is hot, add half the zoodles and cook for 2 minutes, moving them about with tongs, being careful not to break them. Put them in a large bowl and cook the remaining zoodles with an extra tablespoon of oil. Add them to the bowl, add the pesto and cherry tomatoes and toss gently to combine.

7 Thinly slice the chicken. Divide the zoodles between bowls and top with the chicken. Scatter over the basil leaves (if using) and serve the carrot and/or cucumber batons on the side, if desired. Serve the zoodles immediately or they can become soggy.

Continued on page 64

Basil pesto makes about 190 g (6½ oz)

45 g (1½ oz/¼ cup) pine nuts
1 large handful of basil leaves
1 small garlic clove, crushed
60 g (2 oz) coarsely grated
  parmesan
½ teaspoon sea salt
100 ml (3½ fl oz) olive oil

Preheat the oven to 180°C (350°F)/160°C (320°F) fan-forced. Place the pine nuts on a baking tray and toast them in the oven for 5 minutes until light golden. Remove them from the oven and allow to cool for 5 minutes. Put the pine nuts, basil, garlic, parmesan and salt in a food processor and process until finely chopped. With the motor running, add the olive oil in a steady stream until it is incorporated. Any leftover pesto can be stored in the refrigerator for 3–4 days, covered with a thin layer of oil.

Roasted capsicum and parsley pesto makes about 200 g (7 oz)

40 g (1½ oz/⅓ cup)
  walnut pieces
large handful of flat-leaf
  (Italian) parsley leaves
  and stalks
80 g (2¾ oz) roasted red
  capsicum (bell pepper)
  in oil, drained
1 small garlic clove, crushed
½ teaspoon sea salt
45 g (1½ oz) coarsely grated
  parmesan
60 ml (2 fl oz/¼ cup) olive oil

Preheat the oven to 180°C (350°F)/160°C (320°F) fan-forced. Place the walnuts on a baking tray and toast them in the oven for 5 minutes until light golden. Remove them from the oven and allow to cool for 5 minutes. Put the walnuts, parsley, capsicum, garlic, salt and parmesan in a food processor and process until finely chopped. With the motor running, add the olive oil in a steady stream until it is incorporated. Any leftover pesto can be stored in the refrigerator for 3–4 days, covered with a thin layer of oil.

Dairy-free pesto makes about 180 g (6½ oz)

60 g (2 oz) pine nuts
1 large handful of basil leaves
1 small garlic clove, crushed
½ teaspoon sea salt
80–100 ml (2½–3½ fl oz)
  olive oil
2 teaspoons lemon juice

Preheat the oven to 180°C (350°F)/160°C (320°F) fan-forced. Place the pine nuts on a baking tray and toast them in the oven for 5 minutes until light golden. Remove them from the oven and allow to cool for 5 minutes. Put the pine nuts, basil, garlic and salt in a food processor and process until finely chopped. With the motor running, add the olive oil in a steady stream until it is incorporated. Add 80 ml (2½ fl oz/⅓ cup) of oil to start with, and add the remaining tablespoon if necessary. Add the lemon juice to taste. Any leftover pesto can be stored in the refrigerator for 3–4 days, covered with a thin layer of oil.

Note

You can buy a spiraliser tool fairly cheaply, but you can also use a hand-held shredder – the tool that is the shape of a wide peeler, but produces long thin strips rather than one wide peel. Or you can make zoodles using a good old-fashioned knife. Thinly slice the zucchini lengthwise, then stack the slices on top of one another, and thinly slice these to get strips. Try to use medium-sized zucchini, as larger ones may have lots of seeds and be quite watery.

Variation

This recipe can also be made with beef strips. Either use 600–800 g (1 lb 5 oz–1 lb 12 oz) beef strips, or cut beef steak into thin strips, marinate them, then stir-fry them for 2–3 minutes, or until cooked to your liking.

Honey soy chicken with ginger rice and vegetable medley

This is another of my stand-bys. The chicken can be served cold in a salad, in sandwiches for lunch the next day, or threaded onto skewers and barbecued. You can also replace the rice with noodles if you prefer. Baby corn aren't always available; if necessary, swap them out for another of your favourite vegetables or cut slices off blanched corn cobs.

Honey soy chicken

60 ml (2 fl oz/¼ cup)
  soy sauce
2 tablespoons mirin (see
  note on page 55)
1 tablespoon honey
2 teaspoons finely grated
  fresh ginger
1 garlic clove, crushed
600–800 g (1 lb 5 oz–1 lb
  12 oz) boneless, skinless
  chicken breast, preferably
  free-range
1 tablespoon vegetable oil
  (optional)

Ginger rice and vegetable medley

200 g (7 oz) short-grain sushi
  rice or jasmine rice, rinsed
  thoroughly
2 thin slices of fresh ginger
1 tablespoon vegetable oil
2–3 medium carrots,
  peeled, halved and cut into
  thin matchsticks
115 g (4 oz) baby corn, halved
  diagonally
200 g (7 oz) snow peas
  (mangetout), ends trimmed,
  thinly sliced lengthways
1 tablespoon soy sauce

1 For the honey soy chicken, combine the soy sauce, mirin, honey, ginger and garlic in a shallow dish. Cut the chicken breast into two thinner steaks. To do this, place your hand flat on top of the chicken and use a knife to slice through, horizontally. Add the chicken to the dish, turn to coat in the marinade and set aside for at least 10 minutes, or up to 24 hours, turning regularly.

2 Meanwhile, for the rice and vegetable medley, cook the rice in a rice cooker (if you have one) with the slices of ginger. Alternatively, put the rice in a medium saucepan with the ginger and 375 ml (12½ fl oz/1½ cups) of water and bring to the boil. As soon as it boils, cover the pan with a tight-fitting lid, reduce the heat to the lowest setting and cook for 12 minutes. Turn off the heat and leave the rice to steam, still covered, for a further 8 minutes. Do not lift the lid at any time during cooking.

3 Heat a chargrill pan or frying pan over a medium–high heat, adding a little oil if necessary. Remove the chicken from the marinade (reserving the marinade), allowing any excess to drip off. Cook the chicken, in batches if necessary, for 3–4 minutes on each side, or until cooked through – the exact cooking time will depend on the thickness of your chicken. Keep the cooked meat warm while cooking the remaining chicken.

4 Meanwhile, heat 1 tablespoon of vegetable oil in a wok or large frying pan over a medium–high heat. Add the carrots and corn and 1 tablespoon of water and stir-fry for 2 minutes. Add the snow peas and soy sauce and stir-fry for 2 minutes, or until all the vegetables are tender.

5 Just before serving, pour the marinade into the hot wok and bring it to the boil, removing the pan from the heat as soon as it does.

6 To serve, remove the ginger slices from the rice and fluff up the rice with a fork. Divide the rice between bowls and top with the chicken and vegetables, spooning over the sauce. Alternatively, serve the sauce in a jug on the side for those who want it – the sauce is quite strongly flavoured.

Family-friendly massaman chicken and vegetable curry with rice

I got my kids to eat curry by making a very mild massaman curry for my husband and me, then adding some of the sauce to plain chicken for the kids. Pretty quickly they were eating the full curry and I gradually increased the spiciness. It's hard to indicate how much spice paste to use, because all brands are different. Trial and error seems to be the way to go, but to be safe and ensure that your family will eat it, start with less and build up.

200 g (7 oz/1 cup) jasmine rice

2 thin slices of fresh ginger, plus 2 teaspoons finely grated fresh ginger

1 tablespoon vegetable oil

1 garlic clove, crushed

2 teaspoons–1 tablespoon massaman curry paste

400 ml (13½ fl oz) tinned coconut milk

600 g (1 lb 5 oz) boneless, skinless chicken thigh or breast, preferably free-range, cut into bite-sized pieces

2 medium carrots, peeled, halved and cut into thin matchsticks

115 g (4 oz) baby corn, cut into 2 cm (¾ in) pieces

150 g (5½ oz) snow peas (mangetout), ends trimmed, sliced in half lengthways

1 lime

2–3 teaspoons fish sauce

1 teaspoon brown or white sugar

small handful of fresh herbs, such as coriander (cilantro), Thai basil or flat-leaf (Italian) parsley (optional)

1 Rinse the rice well. Cook the rice in a rice cooker (if you have one) with the slices of ginger. Alternatively, put the rice in a medium saucepan with the ginger and 375 ml (12½ fl oz/1½ cups) of water and bring to the boil. As soon as it boils, cover the pan with a tight-fitting lid, reduce the heat to the lowest setting and cook for 12 minutes. Turn off the heat and leave the rice to steam, still covered, for a further 8 minutes. Do not lift the lid at any time during cooking.

3 Heat the oil in a large saucepan over a medium heat. Add the garlic and grated ginger and cook for 30 seconds until fragrant. Add the curry paste and cook, stirring regularly, for 2 minutes, or until fragrant. Add 2 tablespoons of the coconut milk and, using a wooden spoon, scrape the bottom of the pan to dislodge any crusty bits. Add the remaining coconut milk to the pan. Pour 60 ml (2 fl oz/¼ cup) of water into the empty coconut milk tin and swirl it around briefly. Add the water to the pan and bring to the boil.

4 Add the chicken to the coconut milk and simmer, covered, for 15 minutes if using chicken thigh, or for 10 minutes for breast.

5 Add the carrot and corn to the pan and cook, uncovered, for 3 minutes. Add the snow peas and cook for a further 2–3 minutes, depending on how al dente you like your vegetables.

6 Squeeze the juice from the lime and stir 1 tablespoon of the juice into the curry with 2 teaspoons of fish sauce and the sugar. Taste the sauce and add a little extra lime juice, fish sauce or sugar according to your liking – no one of these flavours should dominate. Roughly chop any herbs you are using.

7 Serve the curry over the rice with the herbs scattered over, or serve the herbs on the side so everyone can scatter their own, if desired.

Variations

To make this dish vegetarian, leave out the
chicken and add 500 g (1 lb 2 oz) cubed firm
tofu at the same time as the baby corn. Or
leave out the tofu and add more of your
favourite vegetables. You will also need to
leave out the fish sauce and replace it with
2 teaspoons of soy sauce.

Pork with rice and black beans

This is a sort of pork chilli con carne. I've kept it mild but, if your family likes a bit more spice, feel free to increase the amount of chilli powder and smoked paprika. Tinned black beans are available from the supermarket.

200 g (7 oz/1 cup) basmati rice
pinch of salt
1 tablespoon olive oil
1 onion, finely chopped
2 garlic cloves, crushed
1 small red capsicum (bell pepper), core and seeds removed, cut into 1 cm (½ in) cubes
1 teaspoon ground cumin
½ teaspoon smoked paprika
¼ teaspoon chilli powder (optional)
600–700 g (1 lb 5 oz–1 lb 9 oz) minced (ground) pork, preferably free-range
400 g (14 oz) tinned diced tomatoes
400 g (14 oz) tinned black beans or kidney beans, drained and rinsed
2 corn cobs, husk and silk removed
2 tablespoons finely chopped coriander (cilantro) (optional)

1 Rinse the rice well. Put the rice, 375 ml (12½ fl oz/ 1½ cups) of water and a pinch of salt in a medium saucepan and place it on the stove top, but do not turn on the heat yet.

2 Heat the olive oil in a large deep frying pan or casserole dish over a medium heat. Cook the onion and garlic for 2–3 minutes. Add the capsicum and cook for 1 minute. Add the cumin, paprika and chilli powder (if using) and stir-fry for 1 minute. Increase the heat to high, add the pork and stir, using a wooden spoon, to break up the mince.

3 As soon as you put the pork in the pan, bring the rice to the boil. Once it boils, cover the pan with a tight-fitting lid, reduce the heat to the lowest setting and cook for 12 minutes. Turn off the heat and leave the rice to steam, still covered, for a further 8 minutes. Do not lift the lid at any time during cooking.

4 Continue to cook the pork for 3–4 minutes until it has browned. Add the tomato and beans, season with salt and pepper and stir to combine. Bring to the boil, then reduce the heat and simmer, covered, for 10 minutes.

5 While the pork is cooking, lie the corn cobs on a board, then slice the kernels off each side using a sharp knife. Add the corn kernels to the pan. Simmer for 5 minutes, covered, then remove from the heat.

6 Stir the coriander (if using) through the pork just before serving, or serve it on the side for whoever wants some.

Optional extra

If your kids are fans of avocado and sour cream, serve some mashed avocado and a bowl of sour cream on the side for dolloping on top.

Bibimbap rice bowl

Bibimbap is a Korean dish of a rice bed with lots of delicious toppings. The ingredients list looks long, but many of the ingredients are duplicated. Traditionally, a bibimbap is all about the different toppings and usually includes meat, vegetables and egg, but you could reduce the number and decide if you want it vegetarian, vegan or with meat. Look through the toppings and choose your favourites. What is vital is the rice! I would suggest serving this dish at the weekend, or when you have sufficient time to prepare each topping.

300 g (10½ oz) short-grain sushi rice, or jasmine rice
2 tablespoons vegetable oil
4 eggs
Gochujang chilli sauce (optional; see opposite page)

Soy chicken or beef

2 tablespoons soy sauce
2 teaspoons white sugar
1 tablespoon rice vinegar
2 garlic cloves, crushed
500 g (1 lb 2 oz) boneless, skinless chicken thigh, preferably free-range, or 500 g (1 lb 2 oz) beef steak
1 tablespoon vegetable oil
1 spring onion (scallion), finely chopped

Pickled carrots

125 ml (4 fl oz/½ cup) rice vinegar
55 g (2 oz/¼ cup) white sugar
1 teaspoon sea salt
2 medium carrots

Garlic zucchini

2 zucchini (courgettes)
1 tablespoon vegetable oil
1 garlic clove, crushed

1 Rinse the rice well. Cook the rice in a rice cooker or according to the packet instructions. Get all the other ingredients ready, so each component can be prepared and cooked quickly.

2 For the soy chicken or beef, combine the soy sauce, sugar, rice vinegar and garlic in a shallow dish. Cut each chicken thigh into thirds or the beef into large pieces and add the meat to the dish. Toss to combine and set aside to marinate while preparing the remaining ingredients.

3 Make the pickled carrots (alternatively, you could also just serve raw grated carrots). Put the rice vinegar, sugar and salt in a small saucepan and bring to the boil to dissolve the sugar. Transfer to a medium heatproof bowl. Peel, then shred the carrots using a mandoline or cut them into thin matchsticks (see note). Add the carrot to the pickling liquid, toss to combine and set aside. For a less vinegary flavour, only leave the carrot in the pickling liquid for 5 minutes.

4 Heat 1 tablespoon of vegetable oil in a large frying pan over a medium heat and cook the chicken or beef, in two batches if necessary, for 4–5 minutes on each side, or until just cooked through for the chicken, and 2–3 minutes on each side for the beef. Cut the meat into 1 cm (½ in) slices, then put it in a bowl and combine it with the spring onion. Keep the meat warm until you are ready to serve. Wipe out the pan or wash it if the marinade has stuck to the bottom.

5 Bring a medium saucepan of water to the boil for the sesame green beans. For the garlic zucchini, cut the zucchini in half lengthways, then into 5 mm (¼ in) semi-circles. Heat 1 tablespoon of vegetable oil in the frying pan over a medium heat and fry the garlic for 30 seconds. Add the zucchini and stir-fry for 2–3 minutes, until softened and light golden. Wipe out the pan ready for the eggs.

Note

If you don't want to matchstick the carrots you can just make them into ribbons using a wide vegetable peeler, or you could do this with cucumber instead.

Sesame green beans

150 g (5½ oz) green beans, ends trimmed, cut into 2–3 cm (¾–1¼ in) pieces
½ teaspoon sesame seeds
1 teaspoon sesame oil
2 spring onions (scallions), finely chopped

6 While the zucchini are cooking, make the sesame green beans. Cook the beans in the boiling water for 2 minutes. Drain well, then return them to the pan and toss with the sesame seeds, sesame oil and spring onion.

7 Heat 2 tablespoons of vegetable oil in the frying pan over a medium–high heat and fry all the eggs, ensuring the yolks are still runny.

8 To serve, divide the rice between wide bowls and arrange the different ingredients (except the eggs) in small, neat piles on top. Place a fried egg on top at the end, and serve the gochujang chilli sauce on the side (if using). To eat, add a little sauce, break the egg yolk and mix it into the remaining ingredients.

Recipe image on pages 74 & 75

Gochujang chilli sauce

Gochujang is a very spicy chilli paste, available from Asian grocers and the Asian section of selected supermarkets. Store it in the refrigerator and use it stirred into soup or fried rice, or combined with mayonnaise for a spicy sandwich filling.

2 tablespoons gochujang chilli paste
2 teaspoons white sugar
1 teaspoon sesame oil
1 teaspoon sesame seeds

Combine all the ingredients in a small serving dish with 1–1½ tablespoons of water.

Bacon and pea risotto

Once you've mastered a basic risotto, there are myriad different flavour combinations to try. I've suggested a few below. Ensure your rice is cooked properly – the rice grain should still have a little bite to it when tested, but it shouldn't be hard nor should it be gluggy. White wine is added for extra flavour. You can leave this out if you prefer – just start adding the stock at this point.

1 litre (34 fl oz/4 cups) good-quality chicken or vegetable stock

1–2 tablespoons olive oil

200 g (7 oz) rindless back bacon, roughly chopped

1 onion, finely chopped

2 garlic cloves, crushed

250 g (9 oz) risotto rice, such as arborio or carnaroli

125 ml (4 fl oz/½ cup) white wine (optional)

300 g (10½ oz) broccoli, cut into small florets

155 g (5½ oz/1 cup) peas (defrosted if frozen)

35 g (1¼ oz/⅓ cup) finely grated parmesan

15 g (½ oz) butter (optional)

baby cos (romaine) lettuce, leaves roughly chopped (optional)

250 g (9 oz) cherry tomatoes, quartered (optional)

1 Bring the stock to a simmer in a medium saucepan, cover with a lid and keep at a gentle simmer.

2 Meanwhile, heat 2 teaspoons of the oil in a large deep frying pan over a medium–high heat. Add the bacon and cook for 3–4 minutes, until golden on each side and the bacon has released its fat. Transfer half the bacon from the pan to some paper towel, leaving any oil in the pan.

3 Reduce the heat to medium and add the onion and garlic to the pan – and a little extra oil if necessary – and fry for 5 minutes until softened. Add the rice and stir for about 30 seconds to coat it in the onion mix. Add the wine (if using) and cook for 1 minute, scraping the base of the pan to dislodge any crusty bits. Season with salt and pepper.

4 Start adding the stock, two ladlefuls at a time. After each addition, stir a couple of times, then leave to cook, uncovered. Once the stock has been absorbed add the next two ladlefuls of stock and stir. Continue adding stock in this way until the rice is tender – this will take about 20 minutes. If the stock is used up before the rice is tender, add a little extra water.

5 While the rice is cooking, bring a medium saucepan of water to the boil and cook the broccoli for 2 minutes. Add the peas and cook for a further minute. Drain well.

6 Once the rice is just cooked – it should be tender but still have a tiny bite to it – stir in the broccoli, peas, the reserved bacon, half the parmesan and the butter (if using). Remove the pan from the heat, cover with a lid and leave to sit for 2 minutes.

7 Serve the risotto scattered with the remaining parmesan, accompanied by the cos lettuce and cherry tomatoes, if desired.

Variations

You can replace the bacon with prosciutto, or omit the bacon and add some shredded cooked chicken for the final 5 minutes of cooking. Another idea is to stir through 200 g (7 oz) cooked mashed pumpkin (squash) 2–3 minutes before serving.

Vegetable fried rice with sweet chilli omelette

For 'proper' fried rice some people say you need cold, cooked rice. However, on many occasions when my kids have asked for this dish, there hasn't been a grain of cooked rice to be found anywhere. So I just start from scratch and there have never been any complaints to management! The sweet chilli omelettes may be a bit spicy for younger kids, so leave out the sweet chilli sauce if preferred and make plain omelettes. I've suggested different flavourings – use as many or as few as you like.

300 g (10½ oz/1½ cups) jasmine rice, or about 700 g (1 lb 9 oz) cold cooked rice
1 teaspoon salt
2 corn cobs, husk and silk removed, or 250 g (9 oz/1⅔ cups) frozen corn kernels, defrosted
2 medium carrots, peeled and diced
1 tablespoon vegetable oil
2 garlic cloves, crushed or finely chopped
2 teaspoons finely grated fresh ginger
150 g (5½ oz) snow peas (mangetout), ends trimmed, thinly sliced lengthways
1 tablespoon soy sauce
optional flavourings (see below)

Sweet chilli omelette

2 tablespoons vegetable oil
4 eggs
2 tablespoons sweet chilli sauce (optional)

Optional flavourings

small handful of coriander (cilantro leaves)
1 red chilli (long or short), seeded and cut into thin strips
2 spring onions (scallions), thinly sliced
40 g (1½ oz/¼ cup) unsalted roasted peanuts or cashew nuts, roughly chopped

1 Rinse the rice well. Put it in a medium saucepan with 450 ml (15 fl oz/1¾ cups) of water and the salt and bring to a simmer over a medium heat. Reduce the heat to low. Cook, covered, for 12 minutes, or until tender and all the water has been absorbed. Turn off the heat and let the rice stand, covered, for at least 5 minutes. Once cooked, fork the rice through gently to separate the grains, then tip it onto a tray to cool slightly. If you have time, chill it in the refrigerator – even 10 minutes is fine.

2 While the rice is cooking, prepare the remaining ingredients. If you are using corn cobs, cook them in a saucepan of boiling water for 3–4 minutes. Remove, leaving the water in the pan, and leave to cool for 3–4 minutes. Return the water to the boil in the saucepan and cook the carrot for 3–4 minutes, or until tender, then drain.

3 Lie the corn cobs on a board, then slice the kernels off each side using a sharp knife.

4 For the sweet chilli omelette, heat 2 teaspoons of the vegetable oil in a wok or large frying pan over a medium-high heat. Lightly beat together 1 egg and 1–2 teaspoons of the chilli sauce (if using). Pour the egg mixture into the hot wok, swirl to coat the base of the pan and leave to set – this should take about 1–2 minutes. Once set, carefully loosen the omelette from the pan, tip it out onto a board and roll it up. Repeat with the remaining ingredients to make four omelettes. Cut the omelettes into 1 cm (½ in) slices.

5 Heat 1 tablespoon of oil in the same pan over a medium heat, add the garlic and ginger and stir-fry for 1 minute. Add the snow peas and soy sauce and stir-fry for 1 minute. Add the rice and stir-fry for 2 minutes or, if using cold rice, stir-fry until the rice is piping hot. Stir in the carrot and corn and stir-fry for 1 minute.

6 Remove the pan from the heat and divide the rice between bowls. Top with the sliced omelette and any of your chosen optional flavourings.

Variation

If you would like to add meat to this dish, add 175–350 g (6–12½ oz/1–2 cups) of shredded cooked chicken or leftover roast pork or beef at the same time as the rice, ensuring the meat is piping hot before serving.

MAINS

MEAT DISHES

With recipes such as smoky chicken burgers, beef koftas and slow-cooked lamb, there should be plenty in this section to keep your family smiling – and it's all about options, options, options to keep everyone happy!

4-5 people ⏱ 25 minutes 🔲 about 1 hour 20 minutes

Roast chicken with orange butter rub, roasted vegetables and creamy gravy

Our family absolutely loves roast chicken and I love cooking it! Yes, there might be a few different components to prepare and, yes, it might all get gobbled up in less than 10 minutes, but it's warming, nurturing food that fills the house with delicious cooking smells. Don't be put off by the parsnips; I think kids like them because they are sweet, so they're worth trying with your family.

Chicken with orange butter and gravy

1 orange
30 g (1 oz) softened butter
1 whole chicken, about
   1.2–1.5 kg (2 lb 10 oz–
   3 lb 5 oz), preferably
   free-range
2 thyme sprigs
1 onion, cut into wedges
255 g (9 oz/1⅓ cups)
   frozen peas
1 tablespoon plain
   (all-purpose) flour
80–125 ml (2½–4 fl oz/½ cup)
   pouring (single/light) cream

1 Preheat the oven to 200°C (400°F)/180°C (350°F) fan-forced. Take two flameproof roasting dishes and add 1 tablespoon of olive oil to one for the roasted vegetables. Put both dishes in the oven while the oven is heating. Bring a medium saucepan of water to the boil for the parsnips (if using).

2 For the chicken, finely grate the zest from the orange and combine it with the softened butter in a small dish. Season with salt and pepper. Cut the orange in half. Squeeze the juice from one orange half and cut the other half into two pieces. Using clean fingers, carefully loosen the skin from around the chicken breast (without splitting the skin). Do this by gently wiggling your fingers between the breast and the skin. Spread half the butter between the flesh and the skin. Spread the remaining butter over the outside of the breast and on the legs. Put the orange pieces and half the thyme inside the chicken cavity.

3 Remove the dish without the oil from the oven and put the chicken inside. Arrange the onion around the outside and add the remaining thyme. Add the orange juice and 250 ml (8½ fl oz/1 cup) of water. Roast for 1 hour–1 hour 20 minutes, depending on the weight, spooning the pan juices over the chicken about every 15 minutes and adding up to an extra 250 ml (8½ fl oz/1 cup) of water if the pan juices evaporate too quickly.

Roasted vegetables

1 tablespoon olive oil
3–4 medium parsnips, about
   450–500 g (1 lb–1 lb 2 oz) in
   total, cut into long wedges
   and cored (optional)
4 medium carrots, quartered
   lengthways, then cut in half
   to make batons
800 g (1 lb 12 oz) waxy or
   salad potatoes, cut in half,
   larger ones quartered
4 garlic cloves, unpeeled

4 Meanwhile, for the roasted vegetables, cook the parsnips for 2–3 minutes in the boiling water. Drain well. Put the parsnips, carrots and potatoes in the pre-heated dish with the garlic cloves. Season with salt and toss to combine. Roast for 45 minutes, shaking the pan once or twice during cooking.

5 Once the chicken is cooked – to check, pierce the thigh and check the juices run clear with no sign of pink – transfer it to a warm plate and cover it with foil. Reserve the juices in the roasting dish.

6 If the vegetables are still roasting, increase the heat by 20°C (70°F) to help brown them. Bring a medium saucepan of water to the boil for the peas. To make the gravy, place the chicken roasting dish over a low heat and whisk in the flour, stirring to prevent any lumps. Stir in the cream (the exact amount will depend on how thick you like your gravy) and bring to the boil. Simmer for 2 minutes.

7 Cook the peas for 2–3 minutes, or until tender, then drain. Carve the chicken and serve it accompanied by the roasted vegetables, peas and gravy.

Recipe image on pages 86 & 87

Note

When I make the gravy for this dish I don't skim off the fat, because this will mean removing all the delicious orange butter as well.

Crumbed chicken with roasted vegetables and crispy kale

When you cook kale in the oven, it gets a crisp texture which many kids love, so it is a good way to introduce them to this nutrient-rich vegetable. As an alternative, the crumbed chicken is great with mayonnaise, avocado, tomato and cucumber inside a wrap or tortilla, or just with mayonnaise on the side, for a picnic or afternoon treat or in a lunchbox.

Roasted vegetables

3 tablespoons olive oil
1 red capsicum (bell pepper), core and seeds removed, cut into 2–3 cm (¾–1¼ in) pieces
1 red onion, cut into 1 cm (½ in) wedges
600–800 g (1 lb 5 oz– 1 lb 12 oz) waxy potatoes, cut into 2 cm (¾ in) cubes
1 small bunch (about 200 g/ 7 oz) kale

Crumbed chicken

600–800 g (1 lb 5 oz– 1 lb 12 oz) skinless, boneless chicken breast, preferably free-range
2 eggs
75 g (2¾ oz/1¼ cups) panko breadcrumbs
2 tablespoons finely chopped flat-leaf (Italian) parsley or coriander (cilantro) (optional)
35 g (1¼ oz/¼ cup) plain (all-purpose) flour
2–3 tablespoons olive or vegetable oil

1 Heat the oven to 200°C (400°F)/180°C (350°F) fan-forced. Start with the roasted vegetables. Put 2 tablespoons of the oil in a large roasting dish and put it into the oven to heat up while preparing the vegetables. Once hot, add the capsicum, onion and potatoes to the pan. Season with salt and toss to combine. Roast for 30–35 minutes, or until the potatoes are tender.

2 Meanwhile, slice the leaves off the kale stems and roughly chop. Discard the stems. Put the kale in a large bowl, add 1 tablespoon of olive oil, season with salt and pepper and toss well to coat. Set aside.

3 While the vegetables are roasting, cut each chicken breast into two thinner fillets. To do this, place your hand flat on top of the chicken and use a sharp knife to slice through, horizontally.

4 Set up a crumbing station. Put one of the eggs in a shallow dish and lightly beat. Combine the panko breadcrumbs and herbs (if using) in a bowl and season with salt and pepper, if liked, then tip half onto a large plate. Place the flour on a separate plate.

5 Line a baking tray with baking paper. Dip each piece of chicken first into the flour, then the egg, allowing any excess to drip off. Then dip into the panko breadcrumbs, coating on all sides. Add the second egg and remaining panko as needed – keeping it in two batches prevents the panko breadcrumbs becoming soggy.

6 Once the vegetables have 10–15 minutes left to cook, scatter the kale on top of the vegetables in the pan and roast until crisp. At the same time, cook the chicken. Heat the oil in a large frying pan over a medium heat. Add the chicken pieces (in batches if necessary) and cook for 2–3 minutes on each side until golden and almost cooked through. Transfer the first batch to the lined tray and keep warm in the oven while frying the remaining chicken.

7 Divide the vegetables between plates and add the crumbed chicken.

6 people   10 minutes   2 hours 45 minutes

Slow-cooked lamb shoulder with cannellini beans and hummus

This one-pot dish is perfect for a weekend. You could easily use a slightly larger piece of meat and invite friends or family over to share in the feast, or just enjoy it with your own family. The dish contains cannellini beans, so I often serve it with hummus and bread, rather than with mashed potatoes or rice. However, if you prefer, leave out the cannellini beans and add your choice of carb.

2 tablespoons olive oil
1 large onion, thinly sliced
2 garlic cloves, crushed or finely chopped
1 kg (2 lb 3 oz) boneless shoulder of lamb (if buying bone-in you'll need to buy about 1.3 kg/2 lb 14 oz)
250 ml (8½ fl oz/1 cup) red wine, vegetable stock or water
800 g (1 lb 12 oz) tinned diced tomatoes
1 teaspoon dried oregano
800 g (1 lb 12 oz) tinned cannellini beans, drained and rinsed (optional)
Quick hummus (optional; see opposite page)
green beans, peas or other green vegetable to serve
4–6 large pitta breads, to serve (optional)
small handful of mint leaves, roughly torn (optional)

1 Preheat the oven to 180°C (350°F)/160°C (320°F) fan-forced. Heat the oil in a large flameproof casserole dish over a medium heat. Add the onion and garlic and cook for about 5 minutes, stirring regularly until they are starting to soften.

2 Remove any excess fat from the lamb. Increase the heat to high, push the onions and garlic to one side, add the lamb and cook it for about 10 minutes, turning the meat to brown it on all sides. Add 125 ml (4 fl oz/½ cup) of the red wine, the tomato and oregano and season with salt and pepper. Cover the pan and bring to the boil.

3 Transfer the dish to the oven and cook for 1 hour. Add the remaining 125 ml (4 fl oz/½ cup) of wine and cook for a further hour.

4 Add the cannellini beans to the lamb and cook for a further 30 minutes, or until the meat is very tender. (If you are not using the beans, continue to cook the lamb for 30 minutes.)

5 If you are making the hummus, prepare it at this point. Cook your choice of green vegetable. Cut the breads in half (if using), place them in a stack on a large piece of foil, wrap them up, then warm them in the oven for 5 minutes.

6 With the lamb still in the dish, using two large forks, shred the lamb into smaller pieces and stir it into the sauce. Scatter over the mint leaves (if using) and accompany with the bread and hummus (if using) and the green vegetables.

Variation

For older kids and adults, just before serving I like to stir in about 20 pitted kalamata olives and crumble in about 200 g (7 oz) feta. You could also serve these at the table for people to add if they wish.

Quick hummus

400 g (14 oz) tinned
chickpeas, drained, rinsed
and drained again
2 tablespoons tahini
½ garlic clove, crushed
pinch of sea salt
40–50 ml (1¼–1¾ fl oz) lemon
juice (about the juice of
1 lemon)
40–50 ml (1¼–1¾ fl oz) olive
oil, plus a little extra to serve

Ensure the chickpeas are well rinsed and drained, then put them in a food processor with the tahini, garlic and salt. Process briefly, then, with the motor running, add the lemon juice, 2 tablespoons of water and the oil. Blend until it forms a smooth creamy purée, adding a little extra oil, lemon juice or water if necessary. Spoon the hummus into a bowl to serve. Any leftover hummus can be covered with plastic wrap and stored in the refrigerator for 4–5 days.

Yummy beef patties and wedges

As I explained before, with many of my recipes I like to hide the vegetables – not necessarily so the kids don't know they are eating them, but so the meal is a kind of all-in-one dish – no mucking around with lots of different things on the plate. These patties are full of carrots and zucchini.

6 burger buns
good-quality whole egg
  mayonnaise, or tomato
  sauce (ketchup)
baby cos (romaine) lettuce
  leaves
1 avocado, thinly sliced
2 firm, ripe tomatoes,
  thinly sliced
Red onion relish (optional;
  see opposite page)

Wedges

800 g (1 lb 12 oz) medium-
  large baking potatoes
1½ tablespoons olive oil
1 teaspoon sea salt

Patties

2 medium carrots, peeled
  and finely grated
2 zucchini (courgettes), about
  400 g (14 oz) in total, finely
  grated
600 g (1 lb 5 oz) minced
  (ground) beef
finely grated zest of 1 lemon
2 teaspoons wholegrain
  mustard
1 egg
75 g (2¾ oz/1¼ cups) panko
  breadcrumbs
1 tablespoon finely chopped
  flat-leaf (Italian) parsley
1–2 tablespoons olive oil

1 If you are making the red onion relish, prepare it now so it has time to cool (see recipe on opposite page).

2 For the wedges, preheat the oven to 220°C (430°F)/200°C (400°F) fan-forced and line two baking trays with baking paper. Cut the potatoes into quite thin wedges and divide them between the trays. Drizzle the potatoes with the oil, season with the salt and toss to combine. Bake for 35–40 minutes, shaking the tray once, until golden and cooked through.

3 Meanwhile, for the patties, using a clean tea towel (dish towel) or clean hands, squeeze out any excess liquid from the carrot and zucchini. Put them in a large bowl with the remaining patty ingredients, except the oil, and season with salt and pepper. Using your hands, thoroughly combine the mix, then form it into eight patties about 2 cm (¾ in) thick. Chill in the refrigerator for about 20 minutes, if you have time.

4 Heat 1–2 tablespoons of olive oil in a large frying pan over a medium heat. Cook the patties for 5–6 minutes on each side until golden and cooked through.

5 Just before serving, cut the burger buns in half, place them on a baking tray and warm them in the oven for 3–4 minutes.

6 Spread a little mayonnaise or tomato sauce on the base of each bun, then top with your choice of accompaniments and a patty. Pop on the bun lids and serve. Alternatively, place all the accompaniments on a platter and let everyone make up their own burgers.

Red onion relish

2 tablespoons olive oil
3 red onions, halved and
  thinly sliced
2 teaspoons balsamic vinegar
1 teaspoon brown or caster
  (superfine) sugar
1 teaspoon picked thyme
  leaves (optional)
½ teaspoon sea salt

Heat the oil in a medium saucepan over a medium–low heat. Sauté the onion for 5 minutes, until softened but not browned. Cover the pan with the lid, reduce the heat to low and continue to cook for about 20 minutes, stirring occasionally. Add the vinegar, sugar, thyme (if using) and salt and cook for a further 10 minutes, uncovered, until the onions caramelise. Serve warm or cold. The relish will last about 1 week in the refrigerator and is delicious in sandwiches or as an accompaniment to cold meats.

Note

Chipotle chillies in adobo sauce are available from some supermarkets, delicatessens and specialist food stores. Store leftovers in an airtight container in the refrigerator. You can purée the chillies and sauce before storing to save chopping them each time. They last for months and are great added to casseroles, soups, tacos or mayonnaise.

6 burgers

25 minutes
(plus 1–4 hours marinating)

 12 minutes

Smoky Mexican chicken burgers with avocado and salad

I found introducing chilli to my kids quite easy using chipotle chillies in adobo sauce. Although you can make it really spicy by adding lots, I add just a little bit of chilli, which makes it mildly spicy but also adds a smoky flavour. Buttered corn cobs are a great accompaniment to these burgers.

Chicken burgers

2 tablespoons olive oil, plus extra for chargrilling
1 tablespoon brown sugar
2 tablespoons apple juice
½–1 chipotle chilli in adobo sauce, finely chopped (see note)
2 garlic cloves, crushed
1 teaspoon dried oregano
3 boneless, skinless chicken breasts, preferably free-range
6 panini, milk buns, brioche buns or your favourite burger buns
90 g (3 oz/⅓ cup) good-quality whole egg mayonnaise
50 g (1¾ oz) rocket (arugula) or soft lettuce leaves
2 avocados, thinly sliced

Tomato and cucumber salad

1 tablespoon olive oil
2 teaspoons white-wine vinegar
½ teaspoon honey (optional)
250 g (9 oz) cherry tomatoes, halved or quartered
2 Lebanese (short) cucumbers, diced

Buttered corn cobs

4 corn cobs, husk and silk removed
20 g (¾ oz) butter

1 For the burgers, combine the olive oil, sugar, apple juice, chipotle chilli, garlic and oregano in a bowl and season with salt and pepper. Cut each chicken breast into two thinner fillets. To do this, place your hand flat on top of the chicken and use a sharp knife to slice through, horizontally. Add the chicken and toss to coat. Leave to marinate in the refrigerator for at least 1 hour, or up to 4 hours, turning the chicken every now and then.

2 If you want to warm the buns through before serving, preheat the oven to 180°C (350°F)/160°C (320°F) fan-forced (alternatively, you can warm them on a barbecue). For the tomato and cucumber salad, combine the oil, vinegar and honey (if using) in a large bowl. Season with salt and pepper to taste. Add the tomato and cucumber to the bowl and toss to combine.

3 Remove the chicken from the marinade, allowing any excess to drip off. Brush a barbecue or chargrill pan with oil, then heat to medium–high. Cook the chicken for 5–6 minutes on each side, or until cooked through.

4 For the buttered corn cobs, boil the cobs for 3–4 minutes. Drain well, cut into pieces and rub with a little butter, if liked.

5 Cut the buns in half and warm them in the oven for 3–4 minutes, or on the barbecue (if using).

6 Spread the cut sides of the buns with mayonnaise. Top each base with rocket, then add a piece of chicken and a few slices of avocado. Pop the bun tops on and serve the burgers accompanied by the corn cobs and the salad.

Thai pork patties with noodles

Although this is a main meal, I've separated out the ingredients so you can see what you need for the pork patties alone. I've done this because these patties make a great lunchbox snack and are good to take on a picnic. You can also serve them with steamed rice and stir-fried vegetables.

250 g (9 oz) vermicelli
  noodles
juice of 1 lime
2 teaspoons fish sauce
1½ teaspoons sesame oil
1½ tablespoons vegetable oil
1 teaspoon white or
  brown sugar
2 medium carrots
1 baby cos (romaine) lettuce,
  shredded
small handful of coriander
  (cilantro) leaves (optional)
small handful of mint leaves
  (optional)

Pork patties (makes 16 small patties)

2 zucchini (courgettes),
  about 400 g (14 oz) in total,
  finely grated
2 garlic cloves, crushed or
  finely chopped
2 teaspoons finely grated
  fresh ginger
600 g (1 lb 5 oz) minced
  (ground) pork, preferably
  free-range
1 tablespoon finely chopped
  coriander (cilantro) leaves
  and stems
2 teaspoons fish sauce
2 teaspoons soy sauce
1–2 tablespoons vegetable oil

1 For the pork patties, using a clean tea towel (dish towel) or clean hands, squeeze out any excess liquid from the zucchini. Put the zucchini in a large bowl with the remaining pork patty ingredients, except the oil. Using your hands, combine the mixture thoroughly for 2–3 minutes. Form the mix into about 16 golf ball–sized balls, then flatten them slightly to form small patties. Chill the patties in the refrigerator while preparing the remaining ingredients.

2 Put the noodles in a heatproof bowl, cover with boiling water and leave to soften for 6–8 minutes, then drain, or cook them according to the packet instructions. Rinse under cold running water to prevent the noodles sticking together. Drain well, then, using scissors, cut them into smaller lengths.

3 In a large bowl, combine 1½ tablespoons of the lime juice with the fish sauce, sesame oil, vegetable oil and sugar. Add the noodles and toss to combine. (If your kids prefer plainer food, leave this dressing off their noodles and drizzle it over the adults' noodles at the end.)

4 Peel, then halve the carrots and, using a mandoline or a sharp knife, cut them into very thin matchsticks.

5 Heat the vegetable oil in a large frying pan over a medium heat and cook the patties for about 12 minutes, turning occasionally, until light golden and cooked through.

6 To serve, divide the noodles between four bowls and top with the carrot and lettuce. Add a patty and the fresh herbs, if desired. Alternatively, the noodles, carrot, lettuce, herbs and dressing can be combined, then served with the patties on top.

Beef kofta in pitta pockets with yoghurt dressing and tomato and cucumber salad

You can make these Greek-style beef patties as big or as small as you like – small ones make good lunchbox treats. They are also a great weekend dinner treat and it's still pretty healthy.

4 wholemeal (whole-wheat) pocket pitta breads
small handful of flat-leaf (Italian) parsley leaves, roughly torn (optional)
small handful of mint leaves, roughly torn (optional)

Kofta

1 teaspoon ground coriander
1 teaspoon ground cumin
2 tablespoons olive oil
¾ large red onion, very finely chopped (use the remaining ¼ for the salad)
1½ garlic cloves, crushed or finely chopped (use the remaining ½ clove for the yoghurt sauce)
600 g (1 lb 5 oz) minced (ground) beef
2 tablespoons finely chopped flat-leaf (Italian) parsley
1 tablespoon finely chopped mint leaves

Salad

3 firm, ripe tomatoes, or 250 g (9 oz) cherry tomatoes, diced
2 Lebanese (short) cucumbers, diced
¼ large red onion, thinly sliced
1 lemon
1 tablespoon olive oil

1 For the kofta, heat a medium, dry frying pan over a medium heat. Add the ground coriander and cumin and cook for 1–2 minutes, or until fragrant, shaking the pan regularly. Tip the spices into a large bowl.

2 Heat 1 tablespoon of the oil in the same pan over a medium heat and fry the onion and garlic for 3–4 minutes until softened. Add to the spices in the bowl.

3 Add the beef, parsley and mint to the bowl and season with salt and pepper. Using clean hands, mix thoroughly for 1–2 minutes. Divide the mixture into 8–12 portions, depending on whether you want larger or smaller koftas, then form them into kofta (short, fat sausage) shapes. Don't make them too fat or they will take quite a while to cook. Chill the koftas for 20 minutes if you have time.

4 Preheat the oven to 200°C (400°F)/180°C (350°F) fan-forced and line a baking tray with baking paper. Heat the remaining tablespoon of oil in the frying pan over a medium–high heat and fry the kofta, in batches if necessary, for 4–5 minutes, turning regularly until they are browned all over. Transfer the kofta to the lined tray and finish cooking them in the oven for 8 minutes if smaller, and 10 minutes if larger. Wrap the stack of pitta breads in a piece of foil, then put them in the oven for 3–4 minutes to warm though while the kofta are cooking.

5 Meanwhile, prepare the salad. Combine the tomato, cucumber and onion in a bowl. (If your family prefers not to mix their food, leave them separate and serve the dressing on the side.) Squeeze the juice from half the lemon and cut the remaining half into wedges. Drizzle the olive oil and 2 teaspoons of lemon juice over the salad and toss to combine.

Yoghurt sauce

200 g (7 oz) Greek-style
  yoghurt
1–2 teaspoons lemon juice
½ garlic clove
pinch of sea salt

6 For the yoghurt sauce, combine the yoghurt with the lemon juice, garlic and salt.

7 Combine the parsley and mint (if using) in a separate small bowl. To serve, cut each pitta pocket in half across the middle, then carefully open out each half to form a pocket. Add a spoonful of yoghurt sauce, a kofta and a spoonful of salad. Top with the herbs, if desired, and another dollop of yoghurt.

Fajitas with tomato and avocado salsa

These fajitas are definitely a family favourite, as well as being popular with the neighbourhood kids! I like them because they can accommodate many different likes and dislikes. I put everything out on the table and let each person choose their filling. Whether they want to eat their salad or vegetables inside their tortilla, or serve them separately on the side, that's fine by me, just so long as they eat them at some point. All three options fill 10 large tortillas. However, you can use smaller tortillas and decrease the quantities as required, or make a selection of chicken, beef and tofu – but then you would need to reduce the quantities of each option. My marinade of choice is a surprising one: soy sauce, honey and ginger – it works really well when chargrilled.

your choice of filling option (see box)
2 tablespoons olive oil
2 garlic cloves, crushed
1 red capsicum (bell pepper), core and seeds removed, thinly sliced
8 spring onions (scallions), ends trimmed, cut into 5 cm (2 in) lengths
200–250 g (7–9 oz) sour cream
150 g (5½ oz) coarsely grated cheddar
50 g (1¾ oz) rocket (arugula) leaves or roughly torn cos (romaine) lettuce
10 large (20 cm/8 in) flour or corn tortillas

Marinade

2 tablespoons soy sauce
1 tablespoon honey
1 teaspoon finely grated fresh ginger

Tomato and avocado salsa

2 avocados, diced
3 firm, ripe tomatoes, diced (and seeded if preferred)
2 tablespoons coarsely chopped coriander (cilantro)
1 tablespoon lime juice
2 teaspoons olive oil
1 long red chilli (optional)

1 Preheat the oven to 180°C (350°F)/160°C (320°F) fan-forced. For the marinade, combine all the ingredients in a large bowl. Add your choice of filling (if using seasoned tofu, omit this step) and set aside to marinate for 10 minutes while making the salsa.

2 For the tomato and avocado salsa, put all the ingredients in a medium bowl. Stir lightly to combine and gently mash the avocado.

3 Put 1 tablespoon of the olive oil and the crushed garlic in a bowl, add the capsicum and spring onion and toss to combine.

4 Put the sour cream, grated cheddar and rocket leaves in three separate serving bowls.

5 Wrap the stack of tortillas in foil, then warm them in the oven for 10 minutes (or if heating them in the microwave, follow the packet instructions).

6 Cook your choice of filling, then keep it warm while cooking the vegetables (see the cooking instructions in the box on the opposite page).

7 Wipe out the pan and stir-fry the garlic, capsicum and spring onion for 3–4 minutes, or until tender.

8 To assemble, spread each tortilla with sour cream, then top with your filling of choice, the spring onion, capsicum, rocket, cheese and salsa – or eat it whichever way you wish! Simply roll it up and devour.

Filling options

Before cooking, marinate your chosen filling option as per step 1 of the method on the opposite page.

Chicken: Use 600 g (1 lb 5 oz) thinly sliced boneless, skinless chicken breast (preferably free-range).

To cook, heat 1 tablespoon olive oil in a large chargrill pan or large non-stick frying pan over a medium–high heat and cook the chicken for 5–6 minutes. Stir regularly, until the chicken is cooked through and very slightly blackened.

Beef: Use 600 g (1 lb 5 oz) beef fillet (tenderloin).

To cook, heat 1 tablespoon olive oil in a large chargrill pan or large non-stick frying pan over a medium–high heat and cook the beef for about 3 minutes on each side, or until cooked to your liking, then rest for 2–3 minutes before thinly slicing it. Note that, for speed and convenience, you can use beef stir-fry strips, although I find they release liquid on frying, and it's not as good as slicing your own beef.

Vegetarian: Use 300–400 g (10½–14 oz) firm tofu, or your favourite seasoned firm tofu, cut into 1 cm (½ in) thick slices.

To cook, heat 1 tablespoon olive oil in a large chargrill pan or large non-stick frying pan over a medium–high heat and cook the tofu for about 2 minutes on each side.

FISH DISHES

In this section, you'll find a small selection of fish dishes that will hopefully inspire your kids to love fish forever more. Who can resist a crumbed fish burger, a mashed potato-topped fish pie or delicious fish cakes? As I said in the introduction, starting out with crumbed fish and seafood dishes is a good way to get your kids to overcome their aversion to fish dishes.

Panko-crumbed fish burgers with crunchy coleslaw

It can be hard to get some kids to eat fish – I think these burgers are a great start. Maybe it's the soft texture of fish they don't like, so coating it in breadcrumbs gives a lovely crunch. The crunchy fish fillets can be served without the buns if preferred. I sometimes make double the fish burgers and freeze half, ready for a quick evening dinner. Defrost them in the refrigerator before cooking. The optional spicy chilli and caper mayonnaise is delicious spread on the burgers.

4 of your favourite burger buns
35 g (1¼ oz/¼ cup) plain (all-purpose) flour
1 egg
1 tablespoon milk
60 g (2 oz/1 cup) panko breadcrumbs
600 g (1 lb 5 oz) skinless white fish fillet, about 1.5 cm (½ in) thick – either a single piece that you can portion, or 4 × 150 g (5½ oz) fillets
2–3 tablespoons olive oil
2–3 tablespoons Chilli and caper mayonnaise (see opposite page) or good-quality whole egg mayonnaise

1 Preheat the oven to 180°C (350°F)/160°C (320°F) fan-forced. Cut the burger buns in half and place them on a baking tray. Set aside.

2 For the crunchy coleslaw, combine the red and white cabbage, apple and parsley in a large bowl. In a small bowl, whisk together the mayonnaise, lemon juice and olive oil. Season with salt and pepper and add the mayonnaise mixture to the cabbage mix. Stir thoroughly to combine.

3 Set up a crumbing station. Place the flour on a shallow plate and season it with salt and pepper. Break the egg into a shallow dish and whisk in the milk. Put the panko breadcrumbs on a third plate.

4 Cut the fish into four equal portions, if not already portioned, then remove any remaining pin bones. Dip the fish first in the flour, then the egg, then the panko breadcrumbs, shaking off the excess each time. If you have any excess crumbing ingredients, you can always dip the fish a second time in the egg and panko.

Note

It's just as easy to make these for six people. Just use 6 buns, about 900 g (2 lb) fish, 90 g (3 oz/1½ cups) panko breadcrumbs and two eggs in the coating. The remaining ingredients stay the same.

Crunchy coleslaw

about ¼ (200 g/7 oz) small
   red cabbage, core removed
   and finely shredded
about ¼ (200 g/7 oz)
   small white cabbage,
   core removed and finely
   shredded
1 small green apple, cored and
   cut into thin matchsticks, or
   shredded using a mandoline
2 tablespoons roughly
   chopped flat-leaf (Italian)
   parsley
3 tablespoons good-quality
   whole egg mayonnaise
1 tablespoon lemon juice
1 tablespoon olive oil

5 Heat 2–3 tablespoons of the oil in a large non-stick frying pan over a medium heat. Cook the fish, in a single layer, for 2–3 minutes on each side until golden and cooked through. At the same time, put the burger buns in the oven for 3 minutes to warm through.

6 To serve, spread a little of your choice of mayonnaise on both sides of each bun and add a spoonful of coleslaw. Top with a fish burger, pop on the bun lids and serve immediately while the burgers are hot and crunchy, with any remaining coleslaw on the side.

Recipe image on pages 106 & 107

Chilli and caper mayonnaise

90 g (3 oz/⅓ cup) good-
   quality whole egg
   mayonnaise
½ red bird's eye chilli, seeded
   and finely chopped
1 tablespoon capers, drained,
   rinsed and finely chopped
2 teaspoons lemon juice
2 tablespoons finely chopped
   dill or flat-leaf (Italian)
   parsley

Combine all the ingredients in a small bowl.

Note

You can use just one type of fish, or a good combination is 200–300 g (7–10½ oz) skinless firm white fish, 200–300 g (7–10½ oz) skinless salmon and 100 g (3½ oz) – about 6 – peeled and deveined raw prawns (shrimp).

Lulu's fish pie with peas

This was a favourite of mine as a child and has since become a hit with the next generation of kids including Lulu, my friend's daughter, who this pie is named after. The first time Lulu ate this she declared it one of the most delicious things she had ever eaten! It takes a little bit of putting together, so if you're short on time, make it the day before and chill, then bake on a pre-heated baking tray for 35–40 minutes, ensuring it is thoroughly heated through and piping hot.

800 g (1 lb 12 oz) mashing potatoes, peeled and cut into bite-sized pieces
50 g (1¾ oz) butter
2 tablespoons milk
3 medium carrots, peeled and cut into batons
1 head of broccoli, cut into small florets

Pie filling

3 eggs
700 g (1 lb 9 oz) fish or seafood (see note)
30 g (1 oz) butter
2 tablespoons plain (all-purpose) flour
625 ml (21 fl oz/2½ cups) milk
35 g (1¼ oz/⅓ cup) finely grated parmesan
205 g (7 oz/1⅓ cups) frozen peas, defrosted

1 Preheat the oven to 200°C (400°F)/180°C (350°F) fan-forced. Grease a 1.5 litre (51 fl oz/6 cup) capacity ovenproof dish. Put the potatoes in a large saucepan of salted water and bring to the boil. Reduce the heat and simmer, covered, for about 12–15 minutes, or until the potatoes are tender when pierced with the tip of a knife.

2 Meanwhile, make the pie filling. Cook the eggs in a small saucepan of boiling water for 7 minutes. Drain, then refresh them under cold water. While the eggs are cooking, cut the fish into 1–2 cm (½–¾ in) cubes and devein and cut any prawns into thirds (if using). Peel the eggs, then cut each egg into six wedges.

3 Melt the butter in a large saucepan over a medium heat. Add the flour and whisk to combine. Whisk almost continuously for 2 minutes to cook the flour. Add the milk very slowly, whisking to incorporate the flour each time. Ensure the sauce is smooth, then simmer for 3–4 minutes to thicken the sauce. Remove the pan from the heat and add the parmesan. Season with salt and pepper.

4 Drain the potatoes well. Return them to the saucepan and cook them over a low heat for 30 seconds to evaporate any liquid. For the mash, add 30 g (1 oz) of the butter and the milk. Mash until the potatoes are smooth.

5 Stir the fish and peas into the cheese sauce, then spoon into the baking dish. Tuck the eggs into the sauce. Top with the mashed potato, ensuring the pie is evenly covered. Using a fork, lightly roughen up the topping. Place the baking dish on a baking tray, then cook the pie in the oven for 20–25 minutes, or until the top is golden.

6 While the pie is baking, cook the carrots and broccoli in a large saucepan of boiling, salted water for 4–5 minutes, or until the vegetables are tender. Drain well. Melt the remaining 20 g (¾ oz) of butter in the pan over a low heat. Remove the pan from the heat, add the vegetables and toss to coat them in the butter.

My ultimate fish cakes

These fish cakes are the ultimate comfort food – crunchy on the outside and soft on the inside. If your kids prefer really simple food, when it comes to mixing the fish cakes, divide the mixture before adding the herbs and spring onion, keep theirs very simple and only add the flavourings to the adults' servings.

600 g (1 lb 5 oz) large mashing potatoes, peeled and cut into bite-sized pieces
pinch of sea salt
600 g (1 lb 5 oz) boneless, skinless white fish fillets, such as ling, flathead or cod, or you could also use 600 g (1 lb 5 oz) skinless, boneless salmon fillet
270 ml (9 fl oz) milk
2 tablespoons plain (all-purpose) flour
1 egg
60 g (2 oz/1 cup) panko breadcrumbs or fresh breadcrumbs from day-old bread
2 spring onions (scallions), finely chopped (optional)
2 tablespoons finely chopped flat-leaf (Italian) parsley (optional)
1 tablespoon finely chopped chives (optional)
2–4 tablespoons olive oil

Continued on page 112

1 Bring a full kettle of water to the boil. Put the potatoes in a large saucepan with the salt and just cover with the boiling water. Simmer, covered, for about 15 minutes, or until the potatoes are tender when pierced with a knife. Drain well, then return them to the saucepan over a low heat and cook for 30 seconds to evaporate any liquid. Mash the potatoes until they are smooth – don't add milk or the potato cakes will be too soft.

2 Meanwhile, put the fish in a wide frying pan and cover with the milk (reserving 1 tablespoon in a shallow dish). Bring to a simmer, turn the fish over and simmer gently, covered, for 5 minutes. Remove from the heat and leave the fish to cool and finish cooking in the milk.

3 Meanwhile, for the herb mayonnaise, combine all the ingredients in a small serving dish and season with salt and pepper. (These quantities can easily be halved if you don't think everyone will want the mayonnaise.)

4 Set up a crumbing station. Put the flour in a bowl and season it with salt. Whisk the egg in the dish with the reserved tablespoon of milk, and put the panko breadcrumbs in a third bowl.

5 Remove the fish from the milk and pat it dry with paper towel. Discard the milk. Add the fish to the potatoes and, using two forks, flake it into small pieces. Add the spring onion, parsley and chives (if using) and season with salt and pepper. Combine the mixture gently, then form it into eight fish cakes about 2 cm (¾ in) thick. The mixture will be quite sticky but it should be fine to form the fish cakes. Chill the fish cakes for 30 minutes if you have time, but it's not vital.

Continued on page 112

Herb mayonnaise

120 g (4½ oz/½ cup) good-quality whole egg mayonnaise
1 teaspoon lemon juice
1 teaspoon capers, rinsed and finely chopped (optional)
2 teaspoons finely chopped chives
2 teaspoons very finely chopped flat-leaf (Italian) parsley

Colourful vegetable medley

2 medium carrots, peeled and cut into batons
200 g (7 oz) green beans, ends trimmed
300 g (10½ oz) broccoli, cut into small florets
20 g (¾ oz) butter (optional)

6 Coat each fish cake first in the flour, then the egg, then the panko breadcrumbs, shaking off the excess as you go (see note).

7 Bring a large saucepan of water to the boil for the vegetable medley.

8 Heat 2 tablespoons of the olive oil in a large frying pan, preferably non-stick, over a medium heat. Fry the fish cakes, in batches if necessary, until golden and heated through, for about 4–5 minutes on each side if not previously chilled, or 5–6 minutes if chilled. Add the extra oil if needed. If you are cooking the fish cakes in batches, keep them warm on a lined tray in the oven at a low temperature.

9 Meanwhile, for the vegetable medley, cook the carrot in the saucepan of boiling water for 2 minutes. Add the beans and broccoli and cook for a further 2–3 minutes, or until the vegetables are cooked to your liking. Drain well. Melt the butter (if using) in the same pan over a low heat. Remove the pan from the heat, return the vegetables to the pan and toss to coat them in the butter. Serve the fish cakes accompanied by the vegetable medley and the mayonnaise.

Note

The fish cakes take a little while to prepare, but they can be made a day in advance, then stored in the refrigerator, or made several days in advance and frozen between layers of baking paper. Defrost them completely in the refrigerator before cooking. It's also worth making a double batch and freezing half for another time.

Fish and vegetable bake

This is a very versatile dish because most types of fish and plenty of different vegetables can be used. Instead of potato, you could use sweet potato. You can also add slices of zucchini (courgette) and carrot. The garlic buttered vegetables are a great 'go-to' recipe when you want something a little more exciting than just steamed or boiled vegetables. Tossing green vegetables in a little butter helps our bodies better absorb their vitamins.

2–3 tablespoons olive oil
700–800 g (1 lb 9 oz–
  1 lb 12 oz) medium–large
  potatoes, peeled and
  thinly sliced
2 fennel bulbs
4 × 150–200 g (5½–7 oz)
  skinless fish fillets, such as
  kingfish, barramundi, ling
  or cod
250 g (9 oz) cherry tomatoes

Garlic buttered vegetables

200 g (7 oz) green beans,
  ends trimmed
200 g (7 oz) snow peas
  (mangetout), ends trimmed
20 g (¾ oz) butter
1 garlic clove, crushed
  (optional)

1 Preheat the oven to 200°C (400°F)/180°C (350°F) fan-forced. Grease a large baking tray with about 2 teaspoons of the olive oil, then arrange the potato slices on the tray in a single layer, if possible, or just slightly overlapping, to cover the tray. Drizzle with a little extra oil and season with salt and pepper.

2 Trim the fronds and stalks from the fennel, then cut the bulb in half lengthways. Place the fennel flat on a board, root end towards you, and cut it into slices about 5 mm (¼ in) thick. Arrange the fennel on top of the potatoes and drizzle with a little extra oil. Season with salt and pepper and bake for 25 minutes.

3 While the vegetables are baking, remove any remaining bones from the fish and pat dry. Brush with a little olive oil and season with salt and pepper to taste.

4 Bring a large saucepan of water to the boil for the garlic buttered vegetables.

5 Place the fish on top of the fennel and potatoes and scatter the cherry tomatoes around. Bake for a further 12–15 minutes, or until the fish is just cooked through – the exact cooking time will depend on the thickness of the fish.

6 Meanwhile, cook the beans and snow peas in the saucepan of boiling water for 3–4 minutes, or until tender. Drain well. Melt the butter in the saucepan over a low heat. Add the garlic (if using) and cook for 1 minute. Remove the pan from the heat, return the vegetables to the pan and toss to coat them in the butter.

7 Serve the fish on a bed of the roasted vegetables, accompanied by the buttered vegetables.

VEGETARIAN DISHES

Most of us know we should be including more vegetarian meals in our diet, but it can be hard to know what to offer your family. This chapter will inspire you with ideas such as frittatas, Indian fritters and a delicious tomato, capsicum and egg dish: the North African shakshuka.

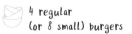
Chickpea and feta burgers with lemon yoghurt dressing

Here's a great meat-free option that hopefully the kids will be excited about. The patties work as burgers, or you can serve them with salad and vegetables. You can replace the lemon yoghurt dressing with a good-quality whole egg mayonnaise. Or try the Chilli and caper mayonnaise on page 105 for adults and the more adventurous eaters.

Chickpea and feta patties

400 g (14 oz) tinned chickpeas, drained, rinsed and drained again
150 g (5½ oz) feta, crumbled
2 tablespoons finely chopped flat-leaf (Italian) parsley
1 teaspoon ground coriander
1½ garlic cloves, crushed
2 tablespoons Greek-style natural yoghurt
60 g (2 oz/1 cup) panko breadcrumbs
1 egg, lightly beaten
2 tablespoons olive oil

To serve

4 burger buns, split
Lemon yoghurt dressing (optional; see below)
good-quality whole egg mayonnaise (optional)
salad leaves (optional)
2 medium carrots, peeled and coarsely grated
1 quantity Red onion relish (optional; see page 93)

1 For the patties, put the chickpeas, feta, parsley, coriander and garlic in a food processor and blend to a rough mixture. Tip the mixture into a bowl and add the yoghurt, panko breadcrumbs and egg and season with salt and pepper. Form the mixture into four patties about 8 cm (3¼ in) in diameter or, alternatively, make eight smaller patties about 6 cm (2½ in) in diameter. Chill the patties in the refrigerator for at least 30 minutes. (If freezing any patties, layer them in between pieces of baking paper and freeze in a freezer bag. Defrost in the refrigerator before cooking.)

2 Heat the olive oil in a large frying pan over a medium heat. Add the patties, in a single layer, and fry them for about 15 minutes, allowing the patties to cook for a few minutes before touching them, to allow a crust to form. Then turn them regularly until they are golden brown and cooked through.

3 While the patties are cooking, if warm buns are preferred, heat them in the oven at a low heat or toast them under a grill (broiler).

4 To assemble, drizzle a little of the lemon yoghurt dressing on the cut sides of each bun, or spread them with some mayonnaise. Top each base with salad leaves and/or carrot (if using). Top with a patty, some red onion relish (if using), another drizzle of dressing and the bun lid.

Lemon yoghurt dressing

70 g (2½ oz) Greek-style yoghurt
1 tablespoon lemon juice
1 tablespoon olive oil
pinch of white sugar
½ small garlic clove, crushed

Combine all the ingredients in a small bowl and season to taste with salt and black pepper.

Corn and capsicum shakshuka with potato bites

This is real comfort food! As well as a hearty dinner dish, this is also great for a light lunch or brunch if you leave out the potatoes and serve the shakshuka on thick slices of buttered sourdough toast.

Potato bites

800 g (1 lb 12 oz) floury potatoes, peeled and cut into 1–2 cm (½–¾ in) cubes
pinch of salt
1 tablespoon olive oil

Shakshuka

1 tablespoon olive oil
1 onion, finely chopped
2 garlic cloves, crushed
1 red capsicum (bell pepper), core and seeds removed, diced
2 corn cobs, husk and silk removed
1 teaspoon ground cumin
800 g (1 lb 12 oz) tinned crushed or diced tomatoes
½–1 teaspoon finely chopped chipotle chilli in adobo sauce (optional; see note on page 94)
4 or 6 eggs (depending on how many eggs each person wants)
small handful of mint leaves to serve (optional)
250 g (9 oz) crumbled feta, or grated cheddar (or use half and half)
100 g (3½ oz) rocket (arugula) to serve (optional)
extra-virgin olive oil or your favourite salad dressing to drizzle (optional)

1 For the potatoes, preheat the oven to 200°C (400°F)/ 180°C (350°F) fan-forced and line a baking tray with baking paper. Bring a full kettle of water to the boil. Put the potatoes in a large saucepan with the salt and just cover with boiling water. Simmer, covered, for 5 minutes. Drain well and shake dry. Place on the baking tray, drizzle with the oil, season with salt (if liked) and roast for 20–25 minutes, or until golden.

2 For the shakshuka, heat the oil in a deep frying pan (about 24 cm/9½ in is a good size) over a high heat. Add the onion, garlic and capsicum and fry for 8–10 minutes, or until slightly charred, stirring occasionally.

3 Lie the corn cobs on a board, then slice the kernels off each side using a sharp knife.

4 Add the ground cumin to the frying pan and fry for 30 seconds, until fragrant. Add the tomato, chipotle chilli (if using) and corn kernels and season with salt and pepper. Reduce the heat and simmer, uncovered, for 10 minutes, or until the sauce thickens slightly.

5 Make four (or six) dents in the tomato sauce in the pan, then crack an egg into each. Cook, covered, for 6–7 minutes, or until the eggs are just set.

6 Scatter the shakshuka with the mint (if using) and the cheese of your choice. Serve accompanied by the potatoes, with the rocket on the side, drizzled with extra-virgin olive oil or salad dressing (if using).

4 people   15 minutes   40 minutes

Roast pumpkin, zucchini and parmesan frittata

This frittata is also good for using up leftover cooked vegetables. Replace the pumpkin and onion with leftover veggies. When adding them to the zucchini, cook them for a few minutes longer to heat through.

2 tablespoons olive oil

300 g (10½ oz) pumpkin (squash), such as butternut or jap

1 red onion, halved and thickly sliced

2 zucchini (courgettes), about 400 g (14 oz) in total

8 eggs

60 ml (2 fl oz/¼ cup) milk

65 g (2¼ oz/⅔ cup) finely grated parmesan

Crunchy salad

50 g (1¾ oz) nuts, such as hazelnuts, pine nuts or walnuts (optional)

2 tablespoons olive oil

2 teaspoons white-wine vinegar

1 baby cos (romaine) lettuce, leaves separated and roughly torn

2 Lebanese (short) cucumbers, diced

1 avocado, diced

1 Put 1 tablespoon of the olive oil in a roasting dish and put the dish in the oven, then heat the oven to 200°C (400°F)/180°C (350°F) fan-forced.

2 Peel the pumpkin and remove any seeds, then cut it into 1 cm (½ in) cubes. Carefully add the pumpkin and onion to the hot oil in the roasting dish and toss to combine. Season with salt and pepper, then bake in the oven for 20–25 minutes, or until the pumpkin is really tender and starting to get a few crisp edges.

3 For the crunchy salad, if you are using the nuts, heat a large frying pan (about 26–28 cm/10¼–11 in is good) over a medium heat. Add the nuts and toast them for 3–4 minutes until golden, shaking the pan to prevent them burning. Put the nuts in a bowl and set aside.

4 Halve the zucchini lengthways, then slice it into 5 mm (¼ in) semi-circles. Once the pumpkin is cooked, heat 1 tablespoon of oil in the large frying pan you used for the nuts over a medium heat and sauté the zucchini for 4–5 minutes, or until light golden, turning the pieces to brown on both sides.

5 Preheat the grill (broiler) to high and move the shelf so the pan will fit under it with about 5 cm (2 in) to spare.

6 Combine the eggs in a large jug or bowl with the milk and three-quarters of the parmesan. Season with salt and pepper – remember that the parmesan may be salty.

Continued on page 122

7 Leave the pan with the zucchini on the heat, add the pumpkin and onion, then spread the mixture evenly in the pan. Add the egg mixture to the pan, distributing it evenly, then leave to cook for 2 minutes. Using a spatula or wooden spoon, gently pull the set egg away from the side, allowing the runny egg to flow into the gaps. Repeat several times around the frittata. Leave to cook for a further 4–5 minutes.

8 Scatter the remaining parmesan over the top of the frittata and place the pan under the grill. (If you have to close your oven door to use the grill and your pan handle is plastic, you will first need to cover it in foil.) Grill (broil) for 3–4 minutes, or until the frittata is puffed and golden. Remember the handle will be very hot when you remove it from the oven.

9 While the frittata is cooking, assemble the crunchy salad. In a large serving bowl, combine the olive oil and vinegar. Add the lettuce, cucumber and avocado and toss to combine. Coarsely chops the nuts (if using) then scatter over the salad.

10 Remove the frittata from the grill, let it sit for a couple of minutes, then shake the pan to loosen the frittata. Either cut the frittata into wedges and serve it from the pan or, if you're feeling confident, hold a clean chopping board on top of the frying pan, then flip the pan over to allow the frittata to drop onto the board. Cut it into wedges and serve accompanied by the crunchy salad.

Variation

Pea and pesto is another delicious frittata combination. Instead of using zucchini, heat 1 tablespoon oil in the frying pan and add the roasted veg. Then add 200 g (7 oz) defrosted frozen peas and stir in 3 tablespoons pesto (see the recipes on page 64). Continue with the egg mixture.

Creamy pea and potato Spanish omelette

Slightly sweet and nutty tasting, manchego cheese is made from sheep's milk. As it becomes more widely known it has become easier to buy, and is now available in the cheese section of many supermarkets. You can easily replace the manchego with cheddar and a little parmesan – I use this combination when I can't get manchego. If you can't find yellow beans, replace them with zucchini (courgette) batons, sliced red capsicum (bell pepper) or extra green beans.

650–750 g (1 lb 7 oz–
   1 lb 11 oz) waxy potatoes,
   peeled and cut into 1–2 cm
   (½–¾ in) cubes
2 tablespoons olive oil
10 eggs, lightly beaten
150 g (5½ oz) crème fraîche or
   sour cream
3 tablespoons coarsely
   chopped flat-leaf (Italian)
   parsley
205 g (7 oz/1⅓ cups) frozen
   peas, defrosted
150 g (5½ oz) manchego or
   cheddar, grated, or use a mix
   of 100 g (3½ oz) cheddar
   and 50 g (1¾ oz) parmesan

Mixed beans in tomato sauce

1 tablespoon olive oil
1 garlic clove, crushed
400 g (14 oz) tinned crushed
   or diced tomatoes
1 teaspoon dried oregano
150 g (5½ oz) green beans,
   ends trimmed
150 g (5½ oz) yellow beans,
   ends trimmed
2 tablespoons finely chopped
   flat-leaf (Italian) parsley
   (optional)

1 Preheat the oven to 180°C (350°F)/170°C (340°F) fan-forced.

2 Cook the potatoes for 10 minutes in boiling, salted water to soften them. Drain well.

3 Heat the olive oil in a non-stick frying pan (about 25 cm/ 10 in in diameter is good) over a medium heat. Add the potatoes and cook them for 8–10 minutes, moving them occasionally, until golden. It's important to get the potatoes golden – it is where lots of the flavour comes from.

4 Meanwhile, combine the eggs, crème fraîche and parsley in a jug and season well with salt and pepper. Ensure the potatoes are in an even layer over the base of the pan, then pour about half the egg mixture over the potatoes. Scatter over the peas and half the cheese, then shake the pan gently. Pour the remaining egg mixture over the top and scatter over the remaining cheese. Shake the pan gently again, so the egg mixture flows into the gaps. Cook for 5 minutes. If your frying pan does not have an ovenproof handle, wrap the handle in foil.

5 Transfer the pan to the oven and cook for a further 15–20 minutes, or until just set and golden. Do not overcook the omelette or it will be dry.

6 While the omelette is in the oven, make the mixed beans in tomato sauce. Heat the oil in a medium or large frying pan over a medium heat and fry the garlic for 30 seconds. Add the tomato and oregano and simmer over a medium–low heat for 10 minutes, or until thickened. Meanwhile, cook the beans in boiling water for 3–4 minutes, or until just tender, then drain.

7 Once the omelette is cooked, remove it from the oven and let it sit for 2–3 minutes. Remember the handle will be very hot. Cut it into wedges and, using a spatula, carefully transfer the wedges to serving plates.

8 Stir the beans and parsley (if using) into the tomato sauce and serve alongside the omelette.

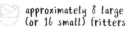
Mild Indian vegetable fritters with minted yoghurt sauce and carrot salad

I've suggested serving these fritters (savoury pancakes) with a minted yoghurt sauce and a grated carrot salad. If your kids prefer things more simple, the fritters can be served accompanied by some raw carrots, cucumber batons and cherry tomatoes.

½ small onion, roughly chopped

1½ garlic cloves, crushed (use the remaining half clove in the yoghurt sauce)

2 teaspoons finely grated fresh ginger

1 green chilli, seeded and roughly chopped (optional)

small handful of coriander (cilantro) leaves

1 egg, separated

180 g (6½ oz/1½ cups) besan (chickpea flour; see notes)

1 teaspoon ground cumin

2 teaspoons ground coriander

1 teaspoon sea salt

2 tablespoons Greek-style yoghurt

225 g (8 oz/1½ cups) frozen peas, defrosted

60 g (2 oz/2 packed cups) baby English spinach leaves, roughly chopped

2–3 tablespoons vegetable oil

Minted yoghurt sauce

140 g (5 oz) Greek-style yoghurt (see notes)

1 tablespoon finely chopped mint

½ garlic clove, crushed

Simple carrot salad

3 medium carrots, peeled and coarsely grated

1 tablespoon olive oil

1 tablespoon coarsely chopped coriander (cilantro)

pinch of sea salt

1 Preheat the oven to 170°C (340°F)/160°C (320°F) fan-forced and line a baking tray with baking paper. Put the onion, garlic, ginger, green chilli (if using), fresh coriander and 1 tablespoon of water in a small blender or spice grinder and blend to a smooth purée. Alternatively, very finely chop all the ingredients and combine, without adding water.

2 Whisk the egg white until firm peaks just form. Put the besan in a large bowl and add the cumin, ground coriander and salt. Add the blended spice paste and the yoghurt. Then add 125 ml (4 fl oz/½ cup) of water and the egg yolk and combine until you have a smooth batter. Stir in the peas and spinach. Then fold in the beaten egg white.

3 Heat 2 tablespoons of the vegetable oil in a large frying pan over a medium–high heat. Drop heaped tablespoonfuls of the batter into the pan (you can make either eight large fritters or about 16 small), then flatten them slightly so they are about 10 cm (4 in) in diameter for large or 5–6 cm (2–2½ in) for small, and cook for 3 minutes on each side until golden. Drain the fritters on paper towel, transfer them to the baking tray and finish cooking them in the oven for 5 minutes. Use the remaining batter to cook more fritters, adding extra oil to the pan as necessary.

4 While the fritters are cooking, make the minted yoghurt sauce by combining all the ingredients in a bowl. Combine the carrot salad ingredients in another bowl – or prepare any other vegetables you want to serve with the fritters.

5 Serve the fritters accompanied by the minted yoghurt sauce and the carrot salad.

Notes ⌄

Besan (chickpea flour)
is available in most
supermarkets on the same
shelf as the other flours.
A 200 g (7 oz) tub of
yoghurt will be sufficient
for both the fritters and the
minted yoghurt.

DESSERTS & AFTERNOON TREATS

Nowadays, a homemade dessert has become more of a treat than an everyday expectation. But sometimes the little bit of extra effort required is worth it, especially when you've got extra time to linger over dinner – and everybody needs something sweet every now and then. This chapter contains a small selection of our favourites: creamy coconut ice cream, my son's fruity berry and lemon curd Eton mess or delectable crumbles. And for Sunday afternoon, head straight for the sweet ricotta fritters – they are truly scrumptious!

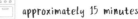

18–20 fritters   10 minutes   approximately 15 minutes

Sweet ricotta fritters with orange-honey syrup

These 'fritters' are so delicious that as soon as I make them, they get gobbled up. The syrup isn't vital, but it does make for a wonderful addition. You could also drizzle the fritters with maple syrup. The kids can help make the batter but an adult will need to do the frying.

250 g (9 oz) firm ricotta
2 eggs, lightly beaten
1–2 tablespoons milk
2 tablespoons caster
   (superfine) sugar, plus
   1 tablespoon extra to serve
finely grated zest of 1 orange
100 g (3½ oz/⅔ cup) plain
   (all-purpose) flour
2 teaspoons baking powder
mild-tasting vegetable oil for
   shallow-frying

Orange-honey syrup (optional)

55 g (2 oz/¼ cup) caster
   (superfine) sugar
2 tablespoons freshly
   squeezed orange juice
   (ensure you grate the
   zest for the fritters before
   juicing)
1 tablespoon honey

1 First, make the orange-honey syrup, if desired. Put the sugar, 60 ml (2 fl oz/¼ cup) of water and the orange juice in a small saucepan and bring slowly to the boil to dissolve the sugar. Add the honey and simmer for 2–3 minutes. Remove the pan from the heat and leave to cool.

2 Preheat the oven to a low heat (170°C [340°F]/160°C [320°F] fan-forced) to keep the fritters warm once cooked. In a large bowl, combine the ricotta, eggs, 1 tablespoon of the milk, the caster sugar and orange zest. If your ricotta is really dry you may need to add the extra tablespoon of milk. Sift the flour and baking powder into the ricotta mix and stir gently to combine.

3 Fill a medium saucepan with oil to a depth of 3–4 cm (1¼–1½ in), then warm the oil over a medium heat. Drop half a teaspoon of batter into the oil, if it bubbles and rises to the surface the oil is hot enough. Carefully drop dessertspoonfuls of mixture into the hot oil (this is easiest done using two spoons, using the second spoon to scrape the mixture off the first). Fry for about 2 minutes, until golden, turning once during cooking and keeping an eye on the oil temperature as you cook each batch. Check when the batter goes into the pan that it doesn't stick to the bottom – if it does, just give it a gentle nudge to dislodge. Remove the fritters from the pan with a slotted spoon, transfer them to paper towel and keep them warm in the oven while cooking the remaining fritters.

4 To serve, sprinkle the fritters with caster sugar and drizzle over the orange-honey syrup (if using).

Coconut ice cream or popsicles

This ice cream is an all-rounder – sophisticated enough for a dinner party but also loved by kids. I infuse the mixture with toasted coconut then sieve out the coconut so you are left with the delicious coconut flavour but no bits of coconut for the kids to complain about! The ice cream can be frozen in a 750 ml–1 litre (25½–34 fl oz/3–4 cup) container or poured into popsicle (ice lolly) moulds.

55 g (2 oz) shredded coconut
500 ml (17 fl oz/2 cups)
    pouring (single/light) cream
250 ml (8½ fl oz/1 cup) milk
110 g (4 oz/½ cup) caster
    (superfine) sugar
4 egg yolks, preferably
    free-range
approximately 6 ice cubes

1 Place a 750 ml–1 litre (25½–34 fl oz/3–4 cup) capacity freezer-proof container or 6–8 popsicle moulds in the freezer to chill. Heat a large, dry frying pan over a medium heat. Add the coconut and toast it for 2–3 minutes, shaking the pan regularly, until the coconut is light golden. Transfer to a large heatproof bowl.

2 Put the cream, milk and half the sugar in a medium saucepan. Heat over a low heat, stirring occasionally, until just below boiling and the sugar has dissolved. Remove the saucepan from the heat and pour the milk mixture over the toasted coconut. Stir to combine, then set aside to infuse for 1 hour. Wash the saucepan.

3 When the milk has infused, place a sieve over the clean saucepan and pour the mixture through, pressing down to extract as much coconut flavour as possible. Discard the coconut. Return the saucepan to the stove and bring to just below boiling point on a medium heat, then set aside.

4 Put the remaining sugar and the egg yolks in a medium bowl and whisk, using an electric mixer, for about 2 minutes, or until the mixture is pale and creamy. Whisk about 125 ml (4 fl oz/½ cup) of the hot cream mixture into the eggs to combine. Add the remaining hot mixture and whisk briefly to combine. Return the mixture to the pan over a low heat for 8–10 minutes, stirring regularly until a custard forms. Do not allow the mixture to boil at any point. The custard is ready when it thickens and coats the back of the spoon. Pour the custard into a medium bowl.

5 Put the ice cubes in a bowl that is larger than the one the custard is in, add about 185 ml (6 fl oz/¾ cup) of water, then sit the bowl of custard on the ice. Cool for about 30 minutes, stirring occasionally to prevent a skin forming.

Note

If you don't have an ice cream machine, pour the mixture into a shallow freezer-proof container and freeze for about 5 hours, or until almost frozen. Blend in a food processor or blender until smooth, then refreeze. Repeat twice, then freeze until frozen – this method prevents ice crystals forming and gives a far creamier texture.

6   Once cooled, pour the mixture into an ice cream machine (see note) and churn according to the manufacturer's instructions. If you are making popsicles, don't churn the ice cream quite so much – you need to still be able to spoon it into the moulds.

7   Either spoon the ice cream into the chilled container, smoothing the top, or pour it into the chilled popsicle moulds and add a popsicle stick to each. Freeze for at least 2 hours, or until firm.

Baked custard with blueberry compote

This is an old-time favourite loved by old and young alike. A custard is a great way to get calcium into kids who don't particularly like milk. The blueberry compote makes for a delicious addition.

4 eggs, plus 2 egg yolks
1 teaspoon natural vanilla
  extract or vanilla bean paste
200 ml (7 fl oz) milk
300 ml (10 fl oz) pouring
  (single/light) cream
70 g (2½ oz) caster (superfine)
  sugar

Blueberry compote

125 g (4½ oz) blueberries
1 tablespoon caster
  (superfine) sugar

1 Preheat the oven to 150°C (300°F)/140°C (275°F) fan-forced. Lightly grease a 1 litre (34 fl oz/4 cup) capacity ovenproof dish that is about 5 cm (2 in) deep. Sit the dish inside a large roasting tin (it needs to be a fair bit bigger than the dish, so there is sufficient room around the dish to remove it once baked, because it will be very hot). Bring a kettle of water to the boil.

2 Put the milk, cream and sugar in a medium saucepan and heat to just below boiling point, stirring to dissolve the sugar.

3 While the milk is heating, put the eggs, egg yolks and vanilla in a large bowl and whisk gently to combine.

4 Slowly pour the milk mixture over the egg mixture and stir gently to combine, then pour the mixture through a sieve directly into the baking dish. Reboil the kettle and pour the boiling water into the roasting tin around the baking dish, to come about halfway up the sides of the dish.

5 Bake for 15–18 minutes, or until the custard is just set – it should still have a bit of a wobble in the middle, as it will continue cooking once out of the oven. Carefully remove the baking dish from the water bath once out of the oven (using a couple of spatulas is one of the easiest ways).

6 Prepare the compote while the custard is cooking. Put the blueberries, sugar and 1 tablespoon of water in a small saucepan over a medium heat and cook for 4–5 minutes, stirring occasionally, until the sugar dissolves. Squash a few of the blueberries while they are cooking to release their juices. Remove the pan from the heat.

7 Leave the custard to sit for 5 minutes, then serve each portion with a spoonful of the blueberry compote. The custard and compote can be served hot or at room temperature.

Greek yoghurt lime and vanilla panna cotta

This panna cotta is pretty fail-safe (if I dare say that!) and is made with Greek yoghurt rather than cream, so you can still call it a pretty healthy dessert.

1½ teaspoons powdered
   gelatine
200 ml (7 fl oz) milk
55 g (2 oz/¼ cup) caster
   (superfine) sugar
finely grated zest of 1 lime
   plus 1½ tablespoons juice
½ teaspoon natural vanilla
   extract or vanilla bean paste
300 g (10½ oz) Greek yoghurt
   (full-fat or low-fat –
   both work)
fresh fruit, such as mango,
   blueberries, strawberries or
   raspberries, to serve

1 Lightly grease four or five 125–150 ml (4–5 fl oz) ramekins or moulds.

2 Put 2 tablespoons of cold water in a small bowl. Sprinkle over the gelatine, stir gently for 10–15 seconds to dissolve the gelatine and leave it to swell and go spongy.

3 Put the milk and sugar in a medium saucepan and bring to a simmer over a low heat, stirring until the sugar dissolves. Using a hand whisk, gently whisk in the gelatine mixture until it has dissolved. Remove the pan from the heat, add the lime zest and set aside to infuse for 3–4 minutes, stirring occasionally.

4 Whisk the vanilla and yoghurt into the milk mix, then stir in the lime juice. Pour the mixture through a sieve into a jug. Divide it between the dishes, place them on a tray and chill them in the refrigerator for 3–4 hours, or until set.

5 Chop your choice of fresh fruit. To serve, gently run a knife around the inside of each mould, place a serving plate on top and turn the panna cotta out. If this doesn't work, dip the moulds briefly in hot water. You can also serve the panna cotta straight from the dishes. Serve accompanied by your choice of fresh fruit.

Note

To get more juice out of a lemon or lime, roll it a few times quite vigorously on a work surface before juicing.

Crunchy fruit crumble

Desserts aren't served nearly as frequently as they were in the past, but there is still a place at the table for a fairly healthy and delicious fruit crumble. I've given options for various fruits, so you can make this whatever the season. It's also worth buying fruit at the height of its season – when it's usually at its best and cheapest – and freezing some. I add nuts to the crumble for added crunch, but they are optional. I also simplify the crumble and stir in melted butter, rather than having to rub in cold butter with your fingertips.

your choice of fruit (see box)
juice of 1 orange

Crumble topping

100 g (3½ oz) unsalted butter
150 g (5½ oz/1 cup) plain
    (all-purpose) flour
75 g (2¾ oz/½ cup) wholemeal
    (whole-wheat) flour
100 g (3½ oz/1 cup) rolled
    (porridge) oats
45 g (1½ oz/lightly packed
    ¼ cup) dark brown sugar
½ teaspoon ground cinnamon
    (optional)
30 g (1 oz/¼ cup) slivered
    almonds (optional)
vanilla ice cream or cream
    (pouring/single/light or
    thickened), to serve

1 Preheat the oven to 190°C (375°F)/170°C (340°F) fan-forced. For the crumble topping, melt the butter. In a large bowl combine the flours, oats, sugar, cinnamon and almonds (if using) until well mixed. Add the melted butter and stir it in until it is evenly distributed. Squash any big lumps with your fingers.

2 Prepare your chosen fruit. If you are using apples, put them in a medium saucepan with 2 tablespoons of water and the orange juice and simmer gently for 5–10 minutes, until they start to soften. If you are using pears that are particularly hard, you might like to cook them in the same way to soften them.

3 Arrange the fruit in the base of a 1.5 litre (51 fl oz/6 cup) capacity ovenproof dish and drizzle over the orange juice, if not already used to soften the fruit. Evenly scatter over the crumble topping. Place the dish on a baking tray and bake for 30–40 minutes, or until the harder fruits, such as apples and pears, are tender.

4 Let the crumble sit for 5 minutes, then serve accompanied by ice cream or cream.

Fruit options

Apple and blackberry: Use 4 cored and sliced or diced apples (peeled or unpeeled) and 125 g (4½ oz) blackberries.

Stone fruit: Use 6 stoned and sliced nectarines or peaches, or 10 stoned and sliced plums or apricots.

Pear and blueberry: Use 4 cored, sliced or diced ripe pears and 125 g (4½ oz) blueberries.

Mixed berries: Use about 700 g (1 lb 9 oz) of a mix of strawberries (quartered), raspberries and blueberries (or use defrosted frozen mixed berries).

Fruity lemon curd Eton mess

I grew up in England and lemon curd on toast was a treat, but my son loves it as a dessert. He's learnt to make lemon curd himself and often makes it on the weekend. Eton mess is a traditional English dessert that consists of a mixture of strawberries, broken up meringue and whipped cream. Here, I've combined lemon curd with berries, crushed meringues and cream for a really delicious treat. You could add some mango and passionfruit – the fruit choice is up to you.

2 eggs, plus 2 egg yolks

110 g (4 oz/½ cup) caster (superfine) sugar

80 g (2¾ oz) chilled unsalted butter, cubed

very finely grated zest and juice of 2 lemons

300 ml (10½ fl oz) thick (double/heavy) cream

500 g (1 lb 2 oz) mixed berries, such as strawberries, raspberries and blueberries

100 g (3½ oz) ready-made meringue (see note)

1 To make the lemon curd, put the eggs, egg yolks and sugar in a medium saucepan (off the heat) and whisk until smooth and combined. Add the butter, lemon zest and juice, place over a low heat and whisk slowly but continuously until the curd thickens. This will take about 6–8 minutes. Do not rush the process by increasing the heat because the eggs will scramble. Remove from the heat. Transfer to a bowl, cover the surface with plastic wrap and chill in the fridge until needed.

2 Whip the cream until soft peaks form.

3 If you are using strawberries, hull them, then roughly chop. Tear the raspberries in half.

4 Crumble the meringue into small pieces and divide it among bowls or place it on a share platter. Spoon over the cream then top with the cooled lemon curd. Scatter over the berries to serve, then dig in.

Note

You can make your own meringues for this and crumble them up, but to be honest, because my son is usually in charge of this dessert, I use the shop-bought mini meringue 'drops'. You could also use meringue nests.

INDEX

ABOUT THE AUTHOR

Katy Holder has always been passionate about cooking and keeping people well fed – reflected in her long and successful career as a food writer and stylist. After having her two kids, she realised she was now responsible for ensuring they grow up with a healthy attitude towards food. Katy has always encouraged Max and Jack (and their friends) to try new flavours, to eat well and enjoy a wide variety of foods. With *Dinner Like a Boss*, her latest book, Katy wants to encourage families to eat well by giving them quick, easy and nutritious meals to serve at dinnertime.

Katy is the author of the *Hungry Campers Cookbook*, *A Moveable Feast* and *Styling Made Simple*. She has been the food director of *Family Circle* magazine, has written the food pages for *marie claire* magazine for several years and has written and styled for most of the leading Australian food magazines and publishers. She also works for Marley Spoon, one of Australia's leading meal kit delivery services.

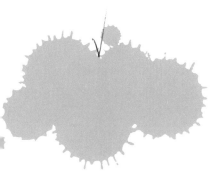

ACKNOWLEDGEMENTS

A lot goes into creating a cookbook, and I am always so touched by the care and sheer hard work that my fantastic publishing team at Hardie Grant put into my books.

So thank you to my publisher, Melissa Kayser. You are a joy to work with and I love that you are always so excited about working with me on my books. Writing a book is like having a baby, you say 'never again', yet here I am with my 4th book thanks largely to your encouragement, Melissa.

To my photo shoot 'Dream Team' Benito Martin, Anna Collett, Jessica Lowe and Simon Collett I say thank you, thank you, thank you! Firstly, to my fantastic photographer, Benito, thank you for being so easy to work with, for getting the best shots out of the kids (and me!) and for working so happily on some long and busy days. To Anna, my editor, who I truly think knows my book better than I do, your attention to detail is phenomenal, you must dream of recipes and layouts! And I must also thank you, Anna, for your amazing watermelon and banana viking hat and spring onion dreadlock skills – who knew you were so talented! To my design manager, Jessica Lowe, always calm, gently steering the design of the shots to get the best from the props and food, much appreciated. To Simon, my photo-chef, thank you for all your hard work during the shoot and for suspending your cheffing skills for the week to do things the way a home cook does, rather than the way a chef does. And, of course, a big thank you for your modelling skills.

Thank you to my designer, Kate Barraclough, I love the design, it really can't be easy coming up with new and interesting ways for yet another cookbook! And thank you to Ariana Klepac for getting the manuscript shipshape and picking up all the tiny details. I must also say a big thank you to the rest of the team at Hardie Grant who I never really get involved with – the sales and marketing teams for example – thank you for caring so much about my book and for getting it out to the world.

Thank you to my gorgeous models Max, Jack, Lulu, Charlotte and Audrey. I love the crazy shots we got and thank you for being so silly.

Thank you to my friends, neighbours and your kids for all your honest feedback on my recipes and for encouraging me to write this book and promising to buy it!

And finally thank you, as ever, to my family Alex, Max and Jack for trying everything I put before you (even Disappointment pizza, Jack) and in most cases loving it and if not, giving me honest feedback!

Katy